COMMUNITY PROFIT

COMMUNITY-BASED ECONOMIC DEVELOPMENT IN CANADA

SUSAN WISMER & DAVID PELL

PUBLISHED BY IS FIVE PRESS

EDITED BY MAUREEN HOLLINGWORTH
COVER DESIGN BY MICHAEL JOHNSON

Financial assistance:
Research:
The research reported in this book was supported in part by grant number MH32382 from the Center for Studies of Metropolitan Problems, (U.S.) National Institute for Mental Health, awarded to the Institute for New Enterprise Development, 17 Dunster St., Cambridge, Massachusetts.

Publication:
Publication of this book is made possible in part by a grant from The Samuel and Saidye Bronfman Family Foundation, under the auspices of Inter Pares, Ottawa, Canada.

Advisory Group: Mark Stiles, Doris Mae Oulton, Art Stinson, Lynn Markell

The many people who gave us support and encouragement:
Erma Stultz, Dal Broadhead, David Wilson, Stephen Graham, David Ross, Stewart Perry, Pat Finucan, Jean-Bernard Daudelin, Ruth and Harry Wismer, Ethel Pell, Doug Kane, Herb Barbolet, Ottawa Community Legal Aid Clinic, and all the folks at Inter Pares.

Community Profit is a non-profit publication. Any surplus revenues will be used to further community economic development work in Canada.

Wismer, Susan, 1951-
Community profit

Includes index.
ISBN 0-920934-02-1

1. Community development - Canada. 2. Community development - Canada - Case studies. 3. Economic development projects - Canada - Case studies.
I. Pell, David, 1948- II. Title.

HN110.Z9C68 307'.0971 C81-094278-X

PUBLISHED BY IS FIVE PRESS
467 RICHMOND STREET EAST
TORONTO, ONTARIO M5A 1R1

Contents

Introduction

The decision to write **Community Profit** developed out of our own experiences as community workers in Eastern Ontario. In recent years, we found that increasing numbers of people wanted to know how to develop locally-based economic projects that could benefit the whole community. In our search for resources and support for these projects, we discovered that the idea of community economic development was not unique to Eastern Ontario. In communities all across Canada, people had been embarking on c.e.d. projects of various kinds, in order to create a greater degree of local control over their communities and economies by reducing local unemployment, raising capital to finance community-based social services and decreasing external dependency.

We also discovered that little had been written about community economic development efforts. In fact, since the 1976 publication of Rollie Thompson's *People Do It All the Time*, only a few articles describing the Canadian experience in community economic development had appeared. People in c.e.d. organizations wanted to know about other communities attempting similar projects, but had no way of finding out about them.

In the fall of 1979, we decided to find a way to document the Canadian search for community self-reliance through economic endeavours. The product of our work, **Community Profit**, has been written as a resource for those who are actively involved in community economic development – either as members of voluntary citizen groups, as paid staff or development workers, or as representatives of supportive educational institutions, government agencies and financial institutions. We also hope that it will be useful to the people who are beginning to study and discuss community economic development – the students, observers and analysts.

Community Profit's contents come from many sources. We started with the experiences and background provided by our years of work in Eastern Ontario. We added three years of study – through reading and visits – of community economic development in Canada and the United States. For example, three weeks spent with people connected with New Dawn Enterprises in Sydney, Nova Scotia, gave us many insights. Then in early 1980, we visited the projects that became the 'meat' of our book. This was a rich and broadening experience. We also benefited greatly from the suggestions, criticisms and voluntary assistance of various friends and acquaintances during the final months of manuscript preparation.

Our book begins with a look at community economic development – what it is and the principles behind it. Then we tell the stories of the seven community projects that provide the basis for much of the rest of **Community Profit.** The unique nature of each project is balanced by some very real and striking similarities. These similarities and differences serve to illustrate the material discussed in the subsequent chapters of the book: chapter three looks at how to get started – what you need to know and what you need to do; chapter four deals with issues of organization – making a plan, choosing strategies and creating a structure; chapter five is an analysis of resources – what they are and how to find them; and in chapters six and seven, we focus on issues related to running your c.e.d. project – financial management and the 'people' part of managing an organization.

At the end of **Community Profit**, you will find the "Index to Resources". Due to the nature of the material covered in this book, there is a lot of 'overlap' – i.e. no chapter is totally self-contained. The 'index' has been devised as a supplement to the book – as a way of simplifying certain aspects of the text by listing and describing related 'resources'. Therefore, whenever you see an asterisk (*) in the text, it refers to a point that can also be found in the index.

Community economic development is not easy to achieve. Support, as our book points out on more than one occasion, is difficult to find. Many of the people who control resources are skeptical about the value of locally-based efforts. Nevertheless, in both small and large communities across Canada, c.e.d. groups are surviving and growing. Faced with the chronic neglect of social and community services, and constantly growing inflation and unemployment rates, many people have decided to take matters into their own hands. In our visits across the country, we were filled with respect for the commitment, energy and discipline that people bring to their community economic development projects.

It is to these people that our book is dedicated. We hope that they will find it a resource. For those who are not yet involved in community economic development, we hope that **Community Profit** helps to draw attention to the efforts of people who are interested in and working towards building a new kind of economic activity – one that is for people, not for profit.

Susan Wismer and David Pell
Ottawa,
October 1980.

1

We'll Do It Ourselves

For some, it's the best way; for others, it's the only way. Any community group that decides to organize and run its own project has made an important decision – its members have become active participants in local development. Rather than being dependent on the decisions of government bodies or large corporations, they have decided to use their own resources to develop a core of self-generated funds.

This is community economic development (c.e.d.). Community economic development projects, like private enterprise, use the 'marketplace' as a source of revenue. They also use public money from government programmes as 'seed money' – or for research and training purposes. However, unlike private enterprise or public programmes, c.e.d. projects organize themselves around the social, economic and cultural problems of their respective communities.

Actually, what we are referring to is something that many Canadian communities have practised for a long time. Canada's earliest co-operatives (the first was established in Stellarton, Nova Scotia in 1861) were far more than just economic institutions. Inspired by Britain's Rochdale pioneers, co-ops – like the British Canadian Co-operative, which was established in North Sydney, Cape Breton in the first years of the twentieth century – gave equal stress to social, cultural and economic initiatives. Their educational committees used every available means to teach community members to control their own lives – to be 'masters of their own destinies' [Coady, 1939]. Early co-operators found their communities being threatened by increasing corporate concentration, and by the export of local resources to remote metropolitan centres. They were convinced that the key to withstanding the onslaught of the 20th century lay in strengthening the cultural, political and economic fabric of local communities.

More than half a century later, the philosophy and the motivation have not really changed. Today's community economic development programmes, however, are not always co-operatives. They take many forms, but whatever their structure, they all belong to the 'third sector' of economic activity. The 'third sector' is neither private enterprise, nor government-sponsored: it includes elements of both. It is also based on an interdependent mixture of social, economic and cultural goals. [Hanratty, 1979: pp. 131-135]

If you put all economic activity into a circle, first you would have to divide it between *formal* and *informal* types of activities. *Formal* activities involve an exchange of money – like paying a mechanic to fix your car. *Informal* activities are productive and have value, but do not require an exchange of money – like fixing the car yourself or doing housework. Then you would divide the circle into sectors: the *private sector* - business interests; the *public sector* – government interests; and the *third sector* – community-based interests.

Log cabin under construction, Mira Community Pasture, Cape Breton.

Of course, it is not really quite so simple. However, it is a fact that most *private* and *public sector* activities are *formal*, and most *third sector* activity is *informal*. Community economic development projects aim to adjust the divisions slightly, so that the size of the *third sector* 'expands', particularly into the *formal* half of the circle.

Some Guiding Principles

"In Canada, there is a definite change of accent among people involved in community development. Many organizations based upon social improvement and community awareness have now faded from the scene – especially with the drying up of available grants. However, lessons have been learned. The most significant lesson learned is that community development requires an economic dimension. At the present time a wide variety of experimental approaches are being tried across the country. Already a remarkable consensus has developed concerning certain key elements involved in community economic development."
– J. Hanratty ed., *New Dawn Enterprises Limited*, Technical Bulletin No. 7, Revised 1979, p. 138.

1. An Integrated Approach to Development

The goals of community economic development projects are never solely economic: they are never limited to just creating jobs or increasing the flow of capital into the community. Nor are the goals solely social or cultural. People who decide to undertake c.e.d. projects believe that development must be integrated if it is to be effective. Just as social problems (such as alcoholism or vandalism), are related to economic problems (like lack of employment opportunities or the absence of a strong business community), so are the solutions to these problems inseparable. Community economic development projects are organized in the interests of the whole community. Accordingly, their goals and strategies relate to the whole community – to its social, economic and cultural elements.

"The plan will be an integrated one taking into account the entire community context (political, social service, educational, cultural, and economic development). . . This integrated and planned approach is unique and innovative and has many implications for other Indian Bands and rural communities across Canada."
– *Nimpkish Integrated Development Approach*, 1975, pp. 16, 18.

"Individual and collective wellbeing depends on the work of three factors; these are the economic, social and cultural factors . . . We believe that any form of expansion must allow man to integrate these three factors. But we are unfortunately convinced that the regional structures of la Haute côte-nord, although effective in their respective fields, do not allow our fellow citizens to integrate these factors in a collective manner . . . The interdependence of the social, economic and cultural areas is given priority in the project and the creation of

jobs and economic development are considered as a means (rather than an end in itself) to a kind of wellbeing."
– Le Groupe Contact, Projet Contact, 1977, pp. 17, 19 .

2. Not for Profit

Community economic development groups must make a profit if they are to survive. However, 'profit' is a 'means', rather than an 'end'. The goal is not simply to make money, but to ensure that the profits are used for the collective benefit of the community.

"In a legal sense, the [community development corporation] is normally non-profit. This means that no member can benefit from the corporation. Membership on the board and committees is on a voluntary, non-paid basis. Any money generated on a particular business venture is then re-invested [sic] in further community projects."
– J. Hanratty ed., *New Dawn Enterprises Limited*, Technical Bulletin No. 7, Revised 1979, p. 134.

3. Not for Personal Gain

Community economic development projects, unlike most traditional small businesses, are not organized to provide personal financial gain for their members. Group members organize their projects to benefit the whole community, and reinvest profits for collective rather than individual gain. Members do of course benefit personally from the projects, but not at the expense of other community members. Their benefits come in the form of goods and services arising from the project.

The Mira Community Pasture Co-op, for example, allows its members to place their animals on the pasture before non-members, but both pay the same fees. There is no expectation that the pasture will be sold at a profit. In effect, the members hold the pasture in trust for the whole community. Their involvement is based on their desire to have a local community pasture – not on the hope that the sale of the improved land will one day make them rich.

4. Local Control

In most cases, people who decide to start a community economic development project have already been involved in other kinds of community efforts. Their common denominator is a feeling that 'real' self-reliance can only be attained through a process of development which is locally controlled.

"It is therefore necessary in order to avoid [falling into the trap of] dependence and [in order to] constantly increase the decision-making power of people over their development, to integrate training programmes at all levels of operation including project and enterprise management."
– Le Groupe Contact, Projet Contact, 1977, p. 47.

They want outsiders to be involved in terms of giving advice and assistance, but recognize that the lasting benefits of a community venture will be much greater, if the final decisions about a project are made within the community by its own members.

5. People Do Have the Capacity to Manage Their Own Affairs

A firm belief in the potential of people is what separates c.e.d. from most other economic development efforts. Community economic development organizations begin with the idea that people have the intelligence and ability to control their own lives. This does not mean that people at the local level always have the necessary skills and knowledge to make good decisions. It does mean, however, that given the opportunity, there are very few people who cannot make good decisions about what is best for them – including decisions about when expert advice is needed. It also does not mean that communities are free from members who are greedy, selfish, corrupt or blind to opinions other than their own. These people do exist, but they are not the majority. Everyone wants what is best for him/herself, but most people understand the benefits of working together in such a venture.

> *"The formula: 'two plus two is five' . . . illustrates the concept of synergy, in which the whole is greater than would be predicted by studying the individual parts."*
> – Promotional flyer, Is Five Foundation.

6. Democracy in Decision-making

In all projects, maximizing community involvement – often through voluntarism – is regarded as essential to continuing success. A broad base of community support is an essential part of the political life of any organization that claims to be working in the interests of the community. Most community enterprises also strive for worker participation in the planning of activities. Some have even attempted to establish businesses that are managed co-operatively by the workers themselves (e.g. Comfort Clothing Services).

7. Small Local Efforts are Viable

In community economic development circles, to say that some project is a 'small local effort', is to praise it. The ideal project is 'local' in all respects: it is owned and managed locally; it is located within its own community; it provides work – paid or voluntary – for local people; it makes use of locally-available resources – both human and material; and it serves local needs by providing required products and services.

Projects like a second-hand clothing exchange (operating in a small village out of a church basement), or a simple food co-op (that sends a borrowed truck once a week to the nearest town to buy bulk goods at wholesale prices), can be better examples of good community economic development than many larger, more impressive projects. Of course, the impact of a small food co-op or second-hand store is quite limited, unless people use this experience to help generate other small projects.

By now, the phrase 'small is beautiful' has been over-used, but it still has special meaning for community economic development efforts. The disadvantages of large projects (what 'large' means varies greatly depending on community size and wealth), need to be weighed carefully against some of the more obvious constraints on profits and services offered by small projects. The larger a project, the more difficult it usually is to manage and finance. Large projects also have difficulty keeping in touch with their community members. For example, maintaining contact with their communities has been a problem for many of the larger, more financially successful co-ops; i.e. they have adopted corporate models of operation that no longer allow for the desired member participation. 'Small' often does turn out to be better.

8. Community ECONOMIC Development

"In the past, a number of political, cultural and social advances have been made, but in large measure the economic strength of Indian communities has not substantially altered. Without the greater ownership or control of the area resources, it is doubtful if one can really consider that Indian people have any greater measure of power to determine their own destiny."
– *Nimpkish Integrated Development Approach,* 1975, p. 36.

Traditionally, community development has focused on social, recreational, cultural and educational projects, leaving economic development to business people and public planners; c.e.d. breaks with that tradition by placing economics at the centre of community development. It does not, however, diminish the importance of social and cultural development by doing so. This is what sets it apart from the regular business community and most economic planners.

Much of our traditional thinking about economic development involves describing social and cultural issues as 'soft', when compared to the 'hard' economic issues. The assumption has always been that a healthy economy automatically means an absence of social and cultural problems. However, a healthy regional or national economy does not automatically create uniformly healthy local economies. The benefits of economic growth tend to be distributed unequally and haphazardly. In times of economic stress, problems of inappropriate and unequal distribution become more pronounced. By working locally, and by giving equal priority to economic, social and cultural goals, c.e.d. organizations try to combat this problem of inequality. The balancing of social and economic needs is a never-ending task in community economic development. How to maintain that balance is an issue of ongoing discussion and experimentation.

"Our social goals determine our activities, but we try to be realistic . . ."
– Member, Is Five Foundation.

"It's hard for the non-business people [board members] to understand costs. But our local business experts – from Queen's [University] and St. Lawrence [College] haven't helped us either. They didn't have good practical expertise – didn't understand small business, couldn't understand the co-operative nature of our work. It's very difficult to keep our business goals together . . . We're here. We're doing it. But sometimes I wonder whether it's possible to run a socially-conscious business in Canada . . ."
– Employee, Comfort Clothing Services.

9. Building Community Self-Reliance

There are many kinds of community economic development projects, but they all have at least one thing in common – goals of greater local self-reliance. Greater self-reliance means different things. It means jobs, but it also means decreasing dependence on outside sources of goods and services, by finding ways to provide such things as food outlets and medical care locally. In addition, greater self-reliance for the project itself is important, so that it is not dependent on outside funding sources. When a community group begins to talk about that kind of self-reliance, it begins a process of community economic development.

"It took us five years to realize the real importance of being self-reliant – the importance of financial planning – finding out how to generate and use money effectively so that we could 'get off the dole' . . ."
– Member, Is Five Foundation.

"Five years ago we depended 90% on grants. Now our revenues are 70% self-generated. Next year they'll be 80 or 90% self-generated."
– Member, Is Five Foundation.

10. It Takes a LONG Time

Community economic development projects are long-term projects. Their impact will not be dramatic or sudden, but will grow slowly over many years. What happens during the first one or two years is usually only a beginning. This does not mean that every c.e.d. group member has to be prepared to commit his/her time to the organization for twenty years. However, it does mean that your organization has to be designed to allow 'new' people to join, 'old people' to leave, and 'leaders' to be changed.

It is absolutely essential to build your philosophy into your organizational structure, since the people will come and go.

"Is Five, it's like we're all floating around separately with a thin rubber band keeping it loosely together – that's our philosophy [that does that] . . . It's the philosophy, because the people keep coming and going, but we're still all together . . ."
– Member, Is Five Foundation.

Many c.e.d. groups are started by one or two 'charismatic' people. It will be very difficult to prevent your organization from revolving around the dynamism and energy of the 'founding leaders', but these people cannot be expected to stay with your organization forever. If it is to survive, your organization must find a base for itself, independent of the leadership qualities of one or two individuals. The best base comes from the shared values and beliefs of your organization – i.e. its guiding principles.

"This is a process – five years is nothing . . ."
– Employee, CCEC.

"I would say to give it a fair shake, you need another ten years . . . Most community projects – I've worked on quite a few – they're a much smaller scope. Four or five months and it's done and over with, whereas, this thing is not going to be finished . . ."
– Member, Mira Pasture Co-op.

For Further Reading:

Coady, M.M., **Masters of Their Own Destiny: The story of the Antigonish movement of adult education through economic co-operation,** New York, Harper & Bros., 1939.

Hanratty, John ed., **New Dawn Enterprises Ltd.: technical bulletin no. 7,** Sydney, Nova Scotia, College of Cape Breton, revised 1979.

Innis, Harold, **Essays in Canadian Economic History**, Toronto, University of Toronto Press, 1956.

Muszynski, Leon, *Jobs Needed: community economic development – a job creation and social development strategy for Metropolitan Toronto*, Social Planning Council of Metropolitan Toronto, March 1979.

Thompson, Rollie, **People Do It All The Time**, Ottawa, Ministry of State for Urban Affairs, 1976.

National Council of Welfare, *Working Together*, Ottawa, Department of National Health and Welfare, 1978.

2

Seven Stories

People are involved in community economic development projects in all parts of Canada. In this chapter, we include the stories of seven communities and their respective projects. There are many others. These seven communities have been chosen, not because they are particularly significant, but because they are typical, and therefore representative of what is happening in terms of c.e.d. in this country.

Comfort Clothing Industries, Kingston.

There's a Mill Again in the Valley

Valley Woollen Mills is a project of the Codroy Valley Rural Development Association. Approximately 3,000 people live in the Codroy Valley, located in south-western Newfoundland. The association represents nine villages, and has sponsored initiatives in health care, transportation, recreation and economic development.

Rural Development Associations (R.D.A.) in Newfoundland are supported by the provincial government, through an agreement with Ottawa's Department of Regional Economic Expansion (DREE). The programme was first started in 1969. Rural areas that could muster the right kind of support (i.e. two representatives from every village area in the region), and were willing to incorporate and to go through the application procedures, were eligible for a grant through the provincial Department of Rural Development. The grant could be used to hire a co-ordinator or for other administrative purposes. The programme got off to a slow start for a variety of reasons, but by 1979, development associations were actively working in thirty-six areas of the province.

"The Rural Development Association? It's the best thing that ever happened to Newfoundland, as far as I'm concerned."
– Member, Codroy R.D.A.

The Codroy Valley was one of the first regions in the province to form a Rural Development Association. It used the grant to hire a co-ordinator to assist in carrying out a wide range of social, educational and recreational projects. By 1975, the Codroy Valley R.D.A. had initiated improvements in transportation systems and in the delivery of health care services to the valley. The association also developed a sports and recreational complex, that in fact serves an area much larger than the Codroy Valley. The time then seemed ripe to take on an economic project – something that would provide local people with jobs.

In earlier times, the valley was a centre for the production of wool, with two mills in operation. The last one, a carding mill, closed during the 1940s. There was also a long tradition – not uncommon in Newfoundland – of home spinning. Most people at one time kept a few sheep and spun their own wool. A significant number of people still keep sheep, but it has become more common to send the wool away to be spun. Sheep farming as a vocation, however, has all but died out in Newfoundland. Based on the valley's tradition of wool production and processing, and an interest in the revitalization of sheep farming, the R.D.A. decided to investigate the possibility of establishing a woollen mill.

In 1975, the R.D.A. obtained funding for a feasibility study from the Department of Rural Development. Members of the R.D.A. visited woollen mills in Prince Edward Island and Nova Scotia, and gathered statistics on sources and markets in Newfoundland. Everything indicated that a mill in Newfoundland could be a viable operation. The Department of Rural Development and DREE then provided another grant to assemble the necessary equipment for the mill.

The next months proved to be very trying. There were many problems and delays. The necessary equipment was not available in Canada, so the R.D.A. hired an American consultant, who travelled through the southern United States buying second-hand machinery for the mill. Transportation costs eventually amounted to more than the cost of the machinery. Customs officials took the machines apart and neglected to put them back together, so that even when the machinery finally arrived in Newfoundland, it was not functional.

Fortunately, the R.D.A. was able to obtain – through the Counselling Assistance to Small Enterprises (CASE) programme of the Federal Business Development Bank* – the services of a Cape Bretoner who had worked in Stanfield's mills for many years. He was able to piece the machines back together. He also trained the nine new employees, who were hired under the federal Canada Manpower in Training programme*, and organized the production floor. By the time the mill opened in June 1977, it was fully operational.

Valley Woollen Mills, Doyles, Newfoundland – first business project of the Codroy Valley Rural Development Association.

Throughout those early days, the co-ordinator of the R.D.A. played an invaluable role. He spent hours in meetings, telephoning, planning, securing resources and filling in gaps whenever necessary. Even with his work, the volunteer members of the R.D.A. found that the mill demanded much more time and effort than they had ever expected.

Since the 1977 opening, the mill has continued to face new challenges. The first lot of wool sent out on the market was of poor quality. This had a negative effect on sales that has only recently been overcome. Provincial statistics on the extent of wool resources in Newfoundland proved to be in error. Two-thirds of the wool for the mill now comes from outside the province; originally it was expected that all raw wool could come from local sources. Another problem arose due to the original composition of the mill's board of directors – i.e. equal representation from the R.D.A. and government. Priorities were so difficult to establish that the board was changed to include only R.D.A. members. Such were some of the mill's 'growing pains'.

> *"We're now employing nine people, and producing 1,000 pounds a week. Between now and spring will tell the tale, just how viable it is . . ."*
> – Manager, Valley Woollen Mills.

During its first three years of operation, the mill received diminishing annual operating grants from the Department of Rural Development. Since the spring of 1980, it has operated without subsidy, as a non-profit enterprise wholly owned by the Rural Development Association. This organizational structure is only temporary. The R.D.A. is eager to 'spin off' the mill as soon as it is financially viable to do so.

> *"Quality is fine now. Quantity, if we can maintain ourselves, is good. Markets are the key – and they're developing. Other R.D.A.s help to promote our project, and the government supports us. The local market is beginning to accept us now. And we're getting inquiries too, from other provinces."*
> – Manager, Valley Woollen Mills.

Valley Woollen Mills, because of assistance from the Department of Rural Development and DREE, has not had to face the capitalization problems that plague most c.e.d. projects. It has, however, had the usual problem of finding technical assistance. The major difficulty has been in finding a manager. The departure of the CASE counsellor left a managerial void, which took many months – and three hiring processes – to fill. Meanwhile, the co-ordinator filled in as manager at the mill.

Once the manager problem was solved, the board was able to concentrate on the role it knows best – that of representing the 'community' side of the mill's operations. The manager, with his business expertise and entrepreneurial attitude, and the board members, with their knowledge of the community's needs and interests have been negotiating a direction for the mill that will hopefully maintain its original social goals – i.e. of providing local employment and fostering the growth of local agriculture, while ensuring its economic success.

> *"We've had close to $500,000 in grants. But it's a small price to pay*

for ten jobs . . . And it [the mill] couldn't be replaced for $1,000,000. It's put us on the map. There's 3,000 people in the Valley who get benefit from that . . ."
– Member, Codroy R.D.A.

Members of the R.D.A. have begun to consider what the best management structure for the mill might be. A co-operative, with the R.D.A. continuing as a partial owner, is one possibility. Other future plans for the mill include weaving recycled wool into blankets. Meanwhile, the R.D.A. has already started its next economic project – an airstrip (construction was due to start in the summer of 1980).

The future of the Codroy Valley Rural Development Association is still uncertain. The provision of necessary technical and managerial assistance to R.D.A. projects will be an ongoing problem. Hopefully, as more and more R.D.A.s in Newfoundland undertake economic projects, a technical assistance pool will be developed: possibly in co-operation with the Memorial University Extension Service, which has provided this type of help in the past.

In addition, the termination of the current DREE agreement in 1981 could mean the end of financial support for Rural Development Associations, and a curtailing of their access to capital. Members of the Codroy Valley R.D.A. have speculated that profits from the mill could help to support their activities, if government support is withdrawn. However, everyone knows that it is unrealistic to expect the mill to be able to generate enough surplus by 1981, capable of paying all the operating costs of the association. Nevertheless, R.D.A. members feel strongly that the benefits of their organization far outweigh the costs, and are confident that they will find a way to continue their work.

"We have a voice now, where before, we didn't. We're organized now. We can control our own affairs, our own development."
– Member, Codroy R.D.A.

Members of the R.D.A. see their organization as the first opportunity that residents of the valley have had to control and promote their own social and economic development. The residents' resourcefulness, independence and historical ties with the region are the greatest assets of the R.D.A., and can be guaranteed not to disappear, no matter what may happen at the government level. However – as is true in other rural communities in Canada – the same independence and ties with tradition that give the people of the valley the determination, patience and tenacity necessary for developmental work, can also mean that people are not always willing to consider new ideas. Members of the R.D.A. know that they must work slowly and thoroughly, if the association is to continue to have the community support so essential for its work.

"Attitude is important. We have to be able to develop local pride and involvement in local efforts, in addition to new businesses . . ."
– Member, Codroy R.D.A.

Contact: "Le développement véritable de la Haute Côte-Nord"

The Development of the Upper North Shore

Contact is a community development corporation serving the upper north shore of the St. Lawrence River, from Tadoussac to Baie-Comeau in Quebec. The population of the region is about 25,000. Contact is based in Les Escoumins. Its goals include the development of new initiatives in agriculture, forestry, tourism and coastal development, communications and small business.

> *"Contact.*
> *It means something.*
> *It is the key.*
> *It is the vital part that will set all the circuits, the gears and the wheels in motion and push the machine forward . . .*
> *Contact is also what happens when two or more people, two or more sources of energy, two or more ideas, two or more ideologies meet . . .*
> *Contact is a series of projects, ideas, achievements that are close enough in time and space for us to have a common hope: the collective and integrated development of la Haute côte-nord."*
> – Le Groupe Contact, Projet Contact, 1977, p. 3.

La Haute Côte-Nord in the province of Quebec has a history of supplying resources to foreign empires. The area around the Saguenay River and east along the north shore of the St. Lawrence River was visited from the eleventh century onwards by whalers – mainly Basque people from France. However, it was not until the mid-nineteenth century, when the American markets for lumber and pulp began to expand, that the area gained many permanent inhabitants. Small villages grew up around the sawmills along the coast. Fishermen from the south shore, Iles de la Madeleine and Newfoundland settled permanently. Today, most of the sawmills are gone, but the villages remain, populated by people who find work – when they can – with the fisheries and the large paper companies that have cutting rights in the region.

> *"Whether it's a question of the private enterprise of finance companies, of governments or of para-public organizations, very often if not always, the decisions that affect the future of the region's citizens are made by others."*
> – Le Groupe Contact, Bilan – An II Rapport Interimaire, 1979, préambule.

La Haute Côte-Nord has never been developed by its own people. Its development has been controlled by outsiders, interested in extracting as much of the area's resources as possible – whether it be whales, wood, minerals or fish. Like many other rural areas in Canada, it has never been self-sufficient or wealthy, although it has helped to make others rich. It has lacked the infrastructure necessary to exploit local resources for local interests. Pockets of resources – such as agricultural land – that are too small to serve world markets, but could adequately provide for a local population, have never developed.

> *"This progress . . . has led to the degradation of the traditional way of life, caused the margination of many 'parishes' and created a lifestyle that can be reduced to six to eight months of work outside the community and four to six months of seasonal unemployment. In the small communities of la Haute côte-nord, this temporary and regular itinerance of a major portion of the active labour force has to some extent paralyzed workers in their own communities (inertia)."*
> – Le Groupe Contact, Projet Contact, 1977, p. 9.

Contact was developed because people wanted to reverse this pattern of dependency. For the people of La Haute Côte-Nord – and many other rural areas in Canada – the task is not to go 'back to the land', but to create a kind of rural community that has never existed before.

> *"The gradual creation of a new social climate encourages the socio-economic self-determination of the communities which are assuming responsibility for their own development. A climate that will tend to bring into harmony the economic, social and cultural aspects of the community's development in order to achieve regional economic expansion is both humane and balanced."*
> – Le Groupe Contact, Projet Contact, 1977, p.20.

Le Groupe Contact began with two LIP grants in December 1976. 'Communiqu'Action' and 'Animation Communautaire' laid the groundwork for 'Projet Contact', through the documentation of the resources of the region, the establishment of networks and links, and the sponsorship of community projects of a social and cultural nature. By the summer of 1977, when these projects ended, the first ideas for 'Projet Contact' had emerged. Information about the experiences of Osmose (Lac St. Jean), New Dawn (Nova Scotia), and American Community Development Corporations* helped to shape those ideas into a preliminary model for the project. At community meetings, and in consultation with local agencies and organizations, a detailed plan was developed.

The essence of Contact's strategy is to provide technical assistance to groups and individuals throughout the region. The aim is to assist in developing the economic, social and cultural infrastructure necessary to deal with problems of unemployment, dependency and poverty. Areas of concentration are agriculture, forestry, tourism and coastal development, communications and small businesses. Mechanisms include: the development of new projects in each area of concentration; the co-sponsorship – through partnerships and consulting contracts – of projects developed outside the group; and the provision of advice and assistance on an individual basis. The focus is on supportive efforts – i.e. on being a catalyst for activities developed by residents of the region.

The plan for Contact was presented to the Department of National Health and Welfare, and an application for a demonstration grant was made in the summer of 1977.* By the end of the following November, the plan was approved. Funds were granted for an initial eighteen month period, with provision for continuation for a period of five years. The funds were allocated to cover the 'overhead' costs of Contact – i.e. the costs of administration and salaries.

When the funding was approved, the provisional co-ordinating committee incorporated a non-profit organization, and reorganized to become the nucleus of a new board of directors. The reconstituted board was designed to be both geographically and sectorally representative. The board's fifteen members come from each of four sub-regions and from various sectors of the community – i.e. a mayors' committee, local co-ops, government organizations, industrial development commissions and the tourist association.

The board (Comité d'Action et de Co-ordination), oversees Contact's staff group (Groupe de Ressources Techniques). The staff includes a co-ordinator, a secretary, an information officer and three development officers; each with a specific area of expertise – agriculture, forestry or economics. These people all assist with proposal-writing, fund-raising, organization, budgeting, marketing and the evaluation of enterprises that fit the philosophy of Contact. For Contact, development must be integrated, initiated by and for local people; it must include co-operative and not-for-profit activities.

In the forestry area, a sawmill has been purchased and is in operation . . .

"Now in its third year Contact wishes to be thought of as an economic development organization of communities and for communities that makes use of the energies of the labour force and the business community . . ."

– Le Groupe Contact, Bilan – An II Rapport Interimaire, 1979, 5.2.5.

Five wood-heated greenhouses are in their first year of full production.

Contact is just beginning its third full year of operation. During its first two years, it made significant progress in four of its five target areas. Communications – the development of local media – has proved to be difficult. In agriculture, however, an ambitious greenhouse and root crop operation is in its first year of production; it involves five wood-heated greenhouses and fifteen acres of vegetables under cultivation. There is also a commercial blueberry operation. In the forestry area: a sawmill has been purchased and is in operation; a co-op forestry project is also in full operation; and assistance has been provided to two other major projects – a second sawmill and a development committee. Courses in marketing and small business management have been offered, and over two hundred people signed up. As well, assistance of various kinds has been given to a number of local small businesses. A major development in the next year will be the construction of a co-op plant for processing fish and seal catches. Contact has involved itself with other co-ops too – including a handcrafts co-op and a food co-op.

Plans for the coming year indicate that the current high level of activity will continue unabated. For le Groupe Contact, the biggest problems are deciding: what to tackle next; maintaining clear priorities based on what local people want; obtaining financing for new projects; and keeping the workload manageable. Like many other people involved in similar projects, staff members and volunteers have to guard against allowing the work to take over their lives. They depend on their resourcefulness, creativity and ability to commit themselves to long hours of hard work. They know that if there is to be a genuine and healthy development effort in their region, the people who live there have to initiate it. No one else knows, and very few people really care, what the needs and desires of the people of la Haute Côte-Nord are. Their success rests on their own determination, patience, strength and willingness to take the risks involved in plunging into the deep and largely unknown waters of community economic development.

> *"In conclusion, it must be mentioned that in recent years la Haute côte-nord has received acknowledgement as a priority area and an experimental area. This could prove useful if the failures of other communities are taken into account, and the working premise is that* ***real development can only come from the community itself."***
> – Le Groupe Contact, Projet Contact, 1977, p. 11.

Community Congress for Economic Change: a Credit Union

CCEC, the Community Congress for Economic Change, is located in Vancouver, British Columbia. It serves co-operative and self-help groups, and individuals who belong to those groups. At present, the CCEC has over 1,000 members, with assets in excess of $600,000.

***The CCEC softball team finished the summer on an optimistic note, with the team victorious** in two of its last eleven games. "Wait until next year."*

*"The first credit unions were formed in Germany in 1869 to enable poor farmers to pool their savings and provide themselves with needed credit at reasonable cost. Today there are over 100 million credit union members worldwide [sic] in countries at all stages of development providing credit to their members and controlled in large measure by the members . . . The Canadian credit union movement began in Levis, Quebec, in 1900 with $26 in deposits. By 1927 there were 159 credit unions with 41,365 members and $12 million in assets. From that time credit unions have grown quickly in Canada and are now a substantial part of the financial system . . . International Credit Union Day, October 19, is an occasion for celebration by more than 8 million Canadian credit union members. They belong to 3,800 credit unions and caisses populaire [sic] across the nation, where they keep close to $20 billion on deposit and where they obtain loans for almost every worthwhile purpose."**

– *CCEC Credit Union Newsletter*, October 1978.

It *is* rather hard to understand why anyone would put hard-earned savings into a banking institution that offers 0% interest. Back in 1974, when a small group of people active in the co-op movement in Vancouver first met to discuss their financial difficulties, no one would have predicted that giving up interest on savings might be a solution.

CCEC developed out of an ongoing need for capital by several community associations and consumer co-ops. People were having trouble raising money to start projects like day care centres, or to make down payments on co-operatively purchased houses. Established lending institutions were reluctant to give community organizations credit, because of their small size and unconventional structures. Some groups were in turn reluctant to use large banks, because of investment policies that were in conflict with their values or beliefs. Several groups, for example, objected to the provision of investment capital to South African corporations by many Canadian banks.

None of the founding organizations had much in the way of savings. In fact, many did not have a continuous pool of money at all – everything that came in, also went out immediately. However, they all had bank accounts, and many of the individuals who were members of the organizations did have some savings. People realized, that by creating their own financial institution, they could pool their individual savings, and gain control over how those savings were used. Their money could be invested in a way that would help them most – i.e. supporting the co-op organizations that they belonged to.

Meetings began in 1974. In due course, a non-profit society – the Community Congress for Economic Change – was incorporated. Its purpose was to organize the credit union. During the next eighteen months, the CCEC researched credit unions. Eventually, they settled on the idea of a no-interest deposit plan. The idea came from Quebec:

"But in the last few years, we have seen interesting results from an idea that was originally brought to Sweden from Quebec. It is a loan and savings institution that instead of interest on savings provides its members with inexpensive goods and services. This is done through other co-operative companies and members can, for example, buy vacations and insurance far

below market prices and get interest-free loans. The aim is to sidestep inflation . . ."
– CCEC *Credit Union Newsletter,* February 1980.

On the way from Quebec to British Columbia, the concept underwent some changes. CCEC's emphasis is less on providing inexpensive services to members and more towards providing the following: ". . . *to support pragmatic alternatives to private capitalism, such as co-ops, and to make credit available to those who really need it and can't get it (i.e. those on fixed incomes, single mothers, and other victims of discrimination)."* [CCEC *Credit Union Newsletter,* February 1980]

The CCEC also organized meetings, did surveys, and sent out information in order to promote understanding of the need for a credit union, designed to serve the needs of the community-based groups in Vancouver interested in social and economic change. In addition, the members of the society had to learn how to run a credit union. An interim board of directors had to draft by-laws, lending policies and a budget, and had to apply to the provincial government for a charter. Not only did members of the CCEC Society have to educate themselves concerning the daily functioning of their credit-union-to-be; they also had to learn how to work with the provincial organization – 'B.C. Central' – and other credit unions.

"We had problems at first, but not since we learned to speak to them in their language . . ."
– CCEC staff member.

The charter was granted after several months. The province's Superintendent of Credit Unions was skeptical – as were most other people – about a no-interest credit union's ability to attract depositors. Finally, in February 1976, with pledges collected from thirty groups and seventy-five individuals, the CCEC credit union started business.

"What's actually happened in the three years since the Credit Union opened its doors? Over a thousand individuals and groups have joined. Deposits at 0% interest have passed $600,000, making us the fastest growing credit union in B.C. [*sic*]. *And with an operating margin of approximately 7% we are running the most expensive credit union in B.C., while simultaneously offering the fewest hours of service, the toughest personal credit policy and, of course, the lowest interest rate on deposits."*
– *CCEC Credit Union Newsletter,* February 1980.

On a day-to-day basis, CCEC operates much like any other credit union. It is a member of the British Columbia Federation and as such, is governed by the provincial charter. It has access to the resources of the 'B.C. Central', and acts as a representative of the Co-operative Trust Company of Canada, receiving deposits on R.R.S.P.s and R.H.O.S.P.s. Chequing and share-savings accounts are also offered.

"Our loans policy is needs-based – women have special difficulties getting loans . . . low-income people can't get credit just because they are on welfare . . . Our default rate is no higher than any other credit

union's. I think it's because we do a fair amount of assistance with loan preparation.People don't have business skills, so we do a lot of financial education. A lot of our time here is spent doing financial counselling . . ."
– CCEC staff member.

Two corner-stones of the CCEC idea are: low interest loans; and public education. The greatest need of this credit union's members is to have easy access to capital. By not paying any interest on deposits, CCEC can pro-

Collective solutions to individual problems – CCEC Credit Union.

vide its members with loans at 8% or 10% (as of February 1980 – at that time, other credit unions and banks were providing consumer loans at 15%). The lower rate is reserved for projects that will make a direct contribution to the co-operative movement. For example, CCEC recently assisted C.A.S. – the Community Alternatives Society – to complete a three-storey, co-op housing complex that will be using solar collectors as a means of providing the necessary energy to heat the water. CCEC was the only financial institution willing to lend C.A.S. the money, thereby enabling them to purchase the material to construct their collectors.

The philosophy of the founding group has been that the awareness of the membership is directly related to the strength of the credit union. If the membership is knowledgeable about the workings of the credit union and co-operatives in general, they will be more committed. CCEC's education committee is largely responsible for putting this principle into action. It co-ordinates the production of the CCEC newsletter, and the organization and/or promotion of relevant learning experiences – e.g. the Economic Planning Conference for Co-operatives, held in May 1979.

CCEC is attempting to be a working alternative to the existing financial system – a resource for the co-operative movement. It performs this function by enabling its member groups to maintain their control over the goods and money they use, by keeping these elements within the local co-operative movement. CCEC itself, because it is a credit union, is organized as a co-operative. Membership is open to:

- any co-operative and self-help group;
- any group whose objectives fall within the philosophy of co-operativism [sic];
- any individual member of one of the above groups;
- the family of any individual member of the Credit Union.

– CCEC Credit Union brochure.

The board of directors and the executive are elected from the membership. In addition, there are several standing committees, including: the education committee; the credit committee, which approves all loans; and the recently formed, long-range planning committee.

> *"A seat on the Board or credit committee is an experience that I would recommend to any member who has the time to come to 2 meetings per month and would like to learn more about the Credit Union. The strength of the credit unions, and CCEC in particular, is dependent on members making the policy and decisons – and not leaving them, increasingly, up to professional managers."*
> – *CCEC Credit Union Newsletter,* November 1978.

> *"The credit committee is a group of nine volunteers who meet weekly in order to discuss and make decisions about the acutal granting of loans to members. We have intereviewed 209 members in the past year, an average of 6 to 8 interviews per meeting. We interview the applicants, discuss their requests, and assess their needs and wants. We try to achieve a balance between the members' needs, their ability to repay the loans, the goals and objectives of the credit union, and our own compassion."*
> –*CCEC Credit Union Newsletter,* February 1978.

The long-range planning committee was formed in May 1979, as one of the outcomes of an economic planning conference. Participants felt that it was time to develop long-term industrial strategies. The committee drew up a list of priorities – areas in which they felt that members of the society should concentrate their enterprise development efforts:

1. They should be oriented to the satisfaction of basic needs – food, clothing and shelter.
2. They should be composed of functioning co-operatives – control should be shared among workers, consumers or clients, and the local community.
3. They should be ecologically responsible – clean and safe.
4. They should be of benefit to all – ownership should be collectively distributed throughout the community.
5. They should be financially sound – "*. . . viable, with good management and markets, since they are to provide us with secure employment, investments and incomes.*"

[*CCEC Credit Union Newsletter,* August/September 1979]

CCEC has enjoyed three very successful years. However, with any community economic development project, its success may bring problems:

> *"Traditionally credit unions fill the needs of working people for consumer home purchase loans. In doing so they bring competitive pressure to bear on private banks to provide better services to broader classes of people, since these people's deposits provide much of the money with which banks finance private industry. It's pretty amazing that credit unions have survived at all in the presence of the bank's massive market coverage, efficiencies of scale, and vastly greater borrowing powers."*
> – *CCEC Credit Union Newsletter,* February 1980.

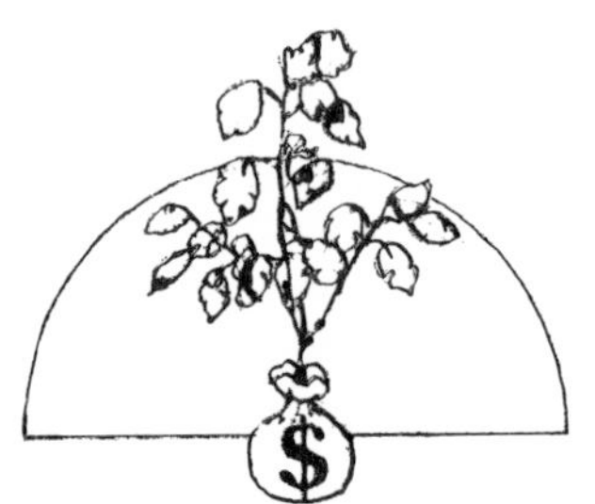

CCEC's hope is to encourage production – the generation of economic goods by members of its community – in addition to consumption. Its ability to support new production, through providing assistance to beginning and expanding businesses, is limited by its small size. Like any small credit union, it faces strong competition and opposition from the larger credit unions and banks.

Most small credit unions respond to competition by striving to become bigger. CCEC, however, was created because its members felt that a small credit union would be better able to attain their goals. CCEC's survival may well be dependent on finding an alternative to growth strategies. It has to develop a way of becoming financially secure, without losing the benefits of being small.

> *"We* ***are*** *small – it's our philosophy to be small . . ."*
> – CCEC staff member.

> *"Most importantly, we must find a way around the tendency for organizations to become more impersonal and harder to influence as they grow larger."*
> – *CCEC Credit Union Newsletter,* October 1978.

New Directions for Women's Work: Comfort Clothing Services

Comfort Clothing Services is a community business located in Kingston, a small city of 60,000 people situated at the eastern end of Lake Ontario. Kingston is a base for government services – educational, penal and military. The largest employers are the federal and provincial governments.

The perils of starting a small manufacturing firm in Canada are enough to discourage all but the most fearless or naive of entrepreneurs: the lack of supportive infrastructure and technical expertise in Canada; the crippling burdens of short production runs and long transportation routes; and competition from imported goods. Many firms, in fact, go bankrupt.* Furthermore, the realities of textile manufacturing industries dictate that the 'sweat shop' image is usually fairly accurate – employee wages are generally low, and the work is repetitive, monotonous and demanding. The success of any small manufacturing firm in Canada demands a high degree of determination, creativity, adaptability and resourcefulness on the part of those involved, as well as a degree of good fortune concerning timing and market conditions. Few survive.

It is not by chance, however, that two of the c.e.d. projects described in this book are manufacturing firms. Manufacturing projects are appealing to c.e.d. groups. Clearly the need exists, especially when you consider that for many manufactured products, there is little or no domestic competition. Furthermore, small manufacturing firms are often labour-intensive, offering a milieu where most, or all, employee training can be done on the job. A firm that can overcome the problems of marketing, capitalization and technical assistance holds the promise of providing a secure and steady source of local employment for its employees. In many regions of Canada, this incentive is more than enough to cause community groups to decide to take on the challenges inherent to this type of project.

> *"We recommend the clothes, not because we're trying to promote a business, but because it's the only product around . . . We just don't manufacture anything* [*aids to the handicapped*] *in Canada . . . I'm sure, if they* [*Comfort Clothing*] *could advertise like Coke, they could sell the world . . ."*
>
> – Physiotherapist, Kingston hospital.

The idea for Comfort Clothing originated in 1975, when St. Lawrence College began to sponsor a store-front operation – a learning centre – located in Kingston's North End. The North End is an area on the fringe of the city, where the original run-down squatters' houses have been replaced, for the most part, by public housing developments that provide subsidized rental housing to low-income families.

Not all the women who came to the learning centre wanted their education in the form of counselling and classes. For some of them, direct work experience seemed a more logical answer to the difficulties of low-income single parenthood. Early in 1976, a committee of these women and staff members from the college approached LEAP* with a request for funding, to study the feasibility of establishing a business that would hire low-income women who were single parents, and who had little or no previous working experience.

The funds were secured and two researchers were hired. By the end of the feasibility study, a plan for Comfort Clothing Services had emerged – a small non-profit manufacturing industry that would produce adaptive clothing for physically handicapped and elderly people, and would employ about fifteen people. The goal of the enterprise was to become a worker-owned business over a three-year period.

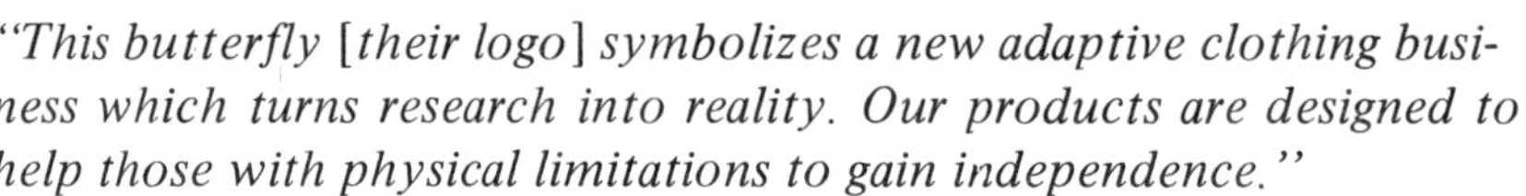

"This butterfly [their logo] symbolizes a new adaptive clothing business which turns research into reality. Our products are designed to help those with physical limitations to gain independence."
– Comfort Clothing Services brochure.

The operating grant for the first year was approved during February 1978. Then the process of acquiring premises, buying equipment and hiring personnel began. There were numerous problems to be overcome. LEAP is designed as a job training/job creation programme, rather than as a funding mechanism for small business development. As a result, its criteria are in some ways not well-suited to the initiation of a small business. For example, finding a suitable location inside the city that would satisfy LEAP's requirement for a one-year lease was difficult. In addition, LEAP's allocation for the purchase of equipment was based on the number of jobs created. This made it difficult to apply the usual practice followed by new manufacturing enterprises, whereby one or two employees are hired in the initial stages of product development, until a marketable product has been established and the first employees are sufficiently experienced. Then, the rest of the firm's employees are brought in (LEAP's criteria have since been changed).

"They haven't been taking the right steps to let us be independent . . . At the end of the funding period, their withdrawal will leave us with no operating capital . . . They could leave us in a serious bind."
– Board member, Comfort Clothing Services.

The most important thing about LEAP, however, is that it does provide a funding base for up to three years, that would otherwise be unavailable to most small, new 'high-risk' enterprises.

In early 1978, Comfort Clothing began operations: with fifteen untrained employees in quarters that were already cramped; with no sales orders; with a product which was still in the first stages of development; and with a goal of employee ownership that no one knew how to realize. By early 1980, however, Comfort Clothing had overcome many of its early problems: a more suitable location had been leased; and, a shiny catalogue was available, displaying high quality clothing, that is both functional and attractive. In addition, a committed group of volunteer board members have consistently provided support and advice. The volunteer members – an accountant, a lawyer and two community college administrators – have been the primary source of knowledge and expertise for the developing enterprise. The core group of experienced employees has been able to provide new workers with the necessary mechanical training and 'c.e.d. orientation'.

At Comfort Clothing, some board members are community volunteers and some are employees. Each year, there have been fewer volunteers and more employees on the board. This year – the third year of operation – marks the first year that employees outnumber the community volunteers on the board.

The temporary assistance of a professional clothes designer, provided through the STEP programme*, has been helping to fill a gap created by several of the first designs (provided by students' research projects), that did not test out. Marketing has also been a major source of difficulty, but with the recent adoption of a national marketing strategy – based on a network of local distributors – the crucial problem of sales appears to be on the road to solution.

However, some problems remain. An early training programme attempted to structure production and personnel policies around two factors: the particular needs of employees who were single parents with no previous work experience and little self-confidence; and, the long-term goal of worker ownership. Such a mode of operation, although suited to a process of skill training, did not turn out to be 'business-like'. As the goals of Comfort Clothing shifted from training to production, the 'business' needs of the enterprise have required – often painful – adjustments and changes in the original policies. There is now a feeling among the workers, managers and board members that the early programme, developed in ignorance of the

Employees produce high quality clothing that is both functional and attractive.

day-to-day requirements of such an enterprise, over-emphasized the 'social' side of things – with the subsequent adjustment adding an extra burden to the already significant struggles involved in forming a small manufacturing firm in Canada.

"Our original emphasis was too much on 'relating', not enough on 'work' – like learning to operate the machines . . . also we [the managers] weren't prepared. We were seen as 'the boss', and we couldn't change that. And twenty years of conditioning that work means bosses, low pay and poor conditions didn't help."
– Manager, Comfort Clothing Services.

"We are beginning to run it more like a business. We have to, and I want us to. . ."
– Employee, Comfort Clothing Services.

With the significant reduction of production and marketing problems, the remaining major challenge for Comfort Clothing is that provided by the concept of employee ownership. With the end of LEAP funding in sight, the question of ownership is becoming more critical. The board members, managers and workers are all concerned with whether or not it is hopelessly idealistic to consider undertaking the unknown problems involved in employee ownership and management, in addition to the challenges that Comfort Clothing already faces. The reluctance of banks and lending institutions to extend a line of credit, or provide loans to non-profit and/or employee-owned enterprises, also presents a major stumbling block.

No matter what model of employee ownership is finally chosen, it will require an even higher degree of determination, flexibility and honesty, than the present situation demands. Regardless, the goal of employee ownership remains, and the people at Comfort Clothing are, for the most part, reluctant to consider alternatives until it has been tried. After all, much has been accomplished already that skeptics probably thought was impossible.

"Who says it can work? Me! I think everybody quite genuinely hopes that it'll work . . ."
– Board member, Comfort Clothing Services.

The Nimpkish Integrated Development Approach: Rebuilding the Land of the Potlatch

*The **Nimpkish Integrated Development Approach** (NIDA) is a programme initiated by the Nimpkish Band. The Nimpkish are members of the Kwakiutl tribe and live at Alert Bay, on an island near the northern end of Vancouver Island in British Columbia. NIDA is administered by the Nimpkish Band Council.*

There is no question that there are basic cultural and social differences between native and non-native communities. With respect to efforts at community economic development, however, there are some significant similarities – i.e. both have to deal with all the problems any small business in Canada has, in addition to those created by their special 'not for profit' status.

Of course, the differences remain. Land claims issues and development of reserve lands, for example, have a unique impact on native efforts at community economic development. In **Community Profit**, we focus on the issues common to native and non-native projects – a viewpoint that is hopefully not misleading. For a full treatment of native community economic development, we will have to wait for a book to be written by native people themselves.

Early anthropologists, who visited the Indian tribes of Canada's mountainous west coast around the turn of the century, found a vibrant culture. The long and distinguished history of the coastal tribes includes, not only the potlatch ceremonies and totem poles described in childrens' history books, but also an economy based on fishing and hunting that was self-sufficient prior to the arrival of the Europeans.

This culture had all but disappeared by the mid-1920s. For the Kwakiutl tribe, living at the northern end of Vancouver Island, things were no better than they were for other coastal tribes. A smallpox epidemic reduced the Kwakiutl population from 10,000 to 3,000 people in less than a decade, and effectively destroyed much of what remained of the already shredded socio-economic fabric of their communities. Since that time, the progress of the Kwakiutl in recovering their cultural, social and economic vitality has been slow, but steady.

> *"In 1974, we were just drifting . . . Everyone wanted to do something other than running to D.I.A. [Department of Indian and Northern Affairs] . . ."*
> – Member, Nimpkish Band Council.

> *"It can no longer be a question of who to blame, but rather how to start another trend . . . another direction."*
> – *Nimpkish Integrated Development Approach*, 1975, p. 13.

In 1975, the Nimpkish Band Council decided that it was time to put some ideas – which had been around for a long time – into practice. It was obvious, despite a good record of political victories in negotiating with federal and provincial governments for native rights, that another kind of initiative was needed. It was the year of 'Habitat', and the promise of a new type of funding for the development of 'model human settlements' – along with a change in band council membership – provided the necessary impetus.

A development worker who had worked with the Nimpkish Band in the past – as a volunteer with the Company of Young Canadians* – was rehired, to assist the band with developing a plan for new ways to achieve more control over their own affairs. The *Nimpkish Integrated Development Approach* was put together in eighteen months: it is a fifty-six page document, outlining a five-year plan for the educational, cultural, social and economic development of the community. Goals and objectives for each year were given in detail. The band council presented the completed plan at a band meeting, where it was voted on and approved by the whole community.

A change in provincial government meant that Habitat funding never did materialize. Nevertheless, the band council decided to proceed with their plans for development, using NIDA as a guide. This represented a significant change in approach – i.e. from an ad hoc method of operation to a co-ordinated strategy, based on long-term goals. The plan called for the band council, while retaining formal control over all development, to create virtually autonomous committees that would direct education, culture and economic development activities.

'Cultural' goals were given immediate attention. Artifacts and historical items used in the potlatch ceremonies had been taken from the band over

A good fishing year is good for everybody.

the years – in some cases by illegal means. For some time, band members had dreamed of reclaiming these items from museums, and building a local cultural centre/museum to house them. The U'Mista Cultural Society, an incorporated non-profit committee of the band council (with an open membership), was formed to help realize this dream, and to oversee the cultural programme. In conjunction with using reclaimed historical pieces as teaching tools, the society has sponsored a programme for teaching young people the old crafts. With the official opening of the new museum in November 1980, U'Mista not only caused a dream to come true; the society now also has a permanent focus for its cultural activities.

"I ask them – Are you an Indian? Do you speak our language? Do you know the myths? Do you know why you're carving what you carve? . . . It's sad – most people don't speak the language. They don't go to school, and they don't learn these things . . ."
– Member, Nimpkish Band Council.

The first educational goals described by NIDA related to gaining control of a large building that once housed a residential school, and locating the funds required to operate it. With the co-operation of the Department of Indian and Northern Affairs, the old school was acquired. It now provides a central facility for a number of educational programmes, including elementary school classes, a marine college, and various programmes offered in co-operation with the local community college. The education committee, although not formally incorporated, operates according to the plan; its biggest job is to provide direction and support to the elementary school.

The distinguishing feature of the NIDA plan is its integration of educational, socio-cultural and economic goals. The focus of the plan is clearly on building self-reliance, through finding means to integrate aspects of traditional culture with present conditions. The plan calls for a high degree of co-operation and entrepreneurship, expressed in terms of concrete local activity.

"Canneries require a lot of capital, so we might start a freezer plant – it's cheaper . . . We've got a consultant looking into it."
– Member, Nimpkish Band Council.

The plan's economic objective described activities which are organized around the use of local resources by band members, in the interests of the whole community. NIDA suggested a number of possible businesses that could be owned by the band council, and employ band members as managers and workers. Feasibility studies established that some of these – such as a laundry – were not viable. However, others – such as a cafeteria/bakery and a lounge – were assessed as being potentially viable, and are now profit-making operations. Profits are allocated to social needs, such as recreational programmes for young people.

"They've never had projects like this, so no one knows how to manage. They need to learn how . . . And the best way, is just to do it, to have these projects . . ."
– Member, Nimpkish Band Council.

Lack of appropriate technical expertise has been a problem that has affected all the economic projects, and even the economic development committee itself. The burden of much of the necessary co-ordinating work has fallen on the shoulders of the band manager, since she is one of the few band members who has the necessary knowledge and expertise in management. Projects have therefore been plagued by a lack of trained management. Not only are there few band members who have the skills and knowledge to provide good management, but there are also very few sources of supportive assistance for on-the-job training.

A shipbuilding operation, purchased in the second year of the development period, is presently inactive due to the lack of a qualified manager. Band council members say that once management resources have been secured, the shipyards will regain their former level of activity and profit. Another venture, a salmon aquaculture programme, was initiated with LEAP funding as an educational programme, in the hope that it would develop into a viable business. After three years, its operations terminated early in 1980, with its viability still in question. The band council has decided not to proceed with this project until additional information and more expertise are available. Meanwhile, a contract with the provincial government to run a 'salmon enhancement programme'* is operating successfully and allowing the work in aquaculture to continue.

Having reached the end of the five-year development period described by NIDA, the band council has decided on a strategy of stabilization.

> *"We have to slow down a bit and take a good look at things . . . We're having problems, so we'd better solve them first, before we take on anything new . . ."*
> – Member, Nimpkish Band Council.

Until some solution to the ongoing problem of too few trained native managers, and/or appropriate management training resources can be developed, the band council is reluctant to take on any new ventures.

Funding is also a problem. As with most c.e.d. efforts, the band's activities suffer from a lack of capital. Although assistance to Indian groups is available through the Department of Indian and Northern Affairs, and through programmes such as Special-ARDA*, it is limited, and shows the same lack of sensitivity to local conditions as do other forms of government programming. For the most part, the Nimpkish have supported their development efforts with assistance from the same provincial and federal sources as are available to non-native groups, and as a result, have experienced the same problems with funding as other c.e.d. groups.

Long-term issues of organization and role are becoming critical in terms of the band council. Whether the band council, which functions like a municipal body, should also own businesses, is becoming an increasingly important question as more projects are initiated. Like many other c.e.d. groups, the council is finding that conventional economic expertise provides it with few clues as to what the alternatives might be. Common corporate models do not allow for the type of community participation that is essential to community economic development. At the same time as it tries to untangle the knot of ownership, the band council has other important long-term problems to face: the need to develop new leadership; land claims questions; and the need at the provincial and federal levels, for a new approach to the management and development of resources in the interests of the small west coast communities.

In spite of the problems to be faced, the achievements of the first few NIDA years provide a basis for optimism. The Nimpkish have accomplished a lot. Their leaders are experienced at making the impossible possible, and they are unafraid of the basic issues involved in building local self-reliance.

> *"Why are things happening here? Because we make the most noise . . . This place has a history of being outspoken . . . This is the home of Jimmy Seaweed."*
>
> – Member, Nimpkish Band Council.

Bringing Farming Back Home: the Mira Community Pasture

The Mira Community Pasture is a co-operative venture with 25 members. It is situated in the Mira Valley, east of Sydney on Cape Breton in Nova Scotia. The valley was first farmed by Acadians, prior to their expulsion in the mid-18th century.

The Mira River is a special place for the people of eastern Cape Breton. The meandering river, the river valley and the low forested hills have been the inspiration of many songs and tales [Fergusson ed., 1958]. Like most of Cape Breton, the Mira has been settled for a long time. It has never been prosperous, but has provided a good living for those who have had the strength to endure its challenging environment. For many years, the Mira area was practically self-sufficient in food, providing the milk and produce for nearby coal towns and fishing villages.

However, those days are long past. Agriculture in Cape Breton has been suffering for many years. The dramatic increases in costs, lack of appropriate government support, and competition from cheap imports have contributed to the rapid disappearance of family farming. Today the majority of farms would not exist without a second income to help cover the costs. Despite the years of difficult times, the spirit for farming still exists. This strong belief in farming as a way of life has been the underlying strength of the Mira co-operative.

> *"It doesn't look in this area of Cape Breton like there's a lot of farming going on, but lots of people are like me – I've still got five animals out there . . ."*
> – Member, Mira Pasture Co-op.

The need for more pasture land is a problem common to most Cape Breton farmers. Cleared land is scarce and expensive, while the alternative of 'clearing' involves more time and money than most farmers could afford. As a result, the idea of a community pasture is an attractive one, because it allows each individual to put his animals on the pasture, while his own land can be used for crops. These crops can then be used for feed during the long winter.

The first public proposal for a community pasture was made to the local county council in 1973. This did not produce any concrete results. In 1974, however, a group started to meet, with the hope of eventually establishing a pasture. Over the course of several meetings an organization was formed, and in the summer of 1975, the Bras D'or Institute of the College of Cape Breton sponsored a 'needs assessment' survey. The report, which clearly indicated the need for a pasture, acted as a catalyst, increasing community interest in the idea. The results of the study were presented to the provincial government in the hopes of getting support. Meanwhile, the Pasture Association was searching for a suitable piece of land.

"The fact that he [the researcher who did the survey] went around and asked questions – that helped a lot. It raised people's interest. They liked him . . ."
– Member, Mira Pasture Co-op.

"I went to each farmhouse twice . . . At first, a lot were very suspicious, unsure of what good this could be . . ."
– Researcher, Mira Pasture Co-op.

"There's little sympathy, trust, or faith in small farmers. Part-time farmers are not really recognized by the government here, but they should be . . ."
– Researcher, Mira Pasture Co-op.

By 1976, it was quite obvious that nothing was forthcoming from government sources. In fact, a piece of land, which the association had requested, was rezoned as a park shortly after the request had been made. The ensuing public furore over the relative merits of parks and pastures was nearly enough to lay the idea of the community pasture to rest for good.

However, the idea of the pasture did not die, and after a period of dormancy, the Pasture Association began to meet again. During one of these meetings, a member suggested that a co-operative be formed. The idea of a co-operative was not new. Cape Breton has a long history of co-operatives, and local residents are well versed as to their value. The members – as individuals – could not afford to purchase adequate amounts of pasture land, but collectively – as a co-op – they could. With this very practical thought in mind, the co-op was established. The cost of shares was set at one hundred dollars. After over three years of effort, the Mira Community Pasture had become a 'project', and was entering a new stage of development.

A 40x100 foot barn has been constructed of materials – poles and stone – from the pasture.

From the outset it was decided that the group would be kept small (25 members), each owning from one to five shares, and having one vote. The executive was to be elected from the membership, but the work-load was to be shared equally. Once again, the group had to search for a suitable site. The share capital contributed by the members, together with a loan signed for by the members, enabled the purchase of the first fifty acres in 1978. By early 1980, the co-op had acquired and fenced 440 acres, and was in the process of adding an additional 160 acres. The members of the co-op also obtained an interest-free loan from the Cape Breton Development Corporation (DEVCO)*, that assisted them in purchasing the land. A land-clearing grant from the provincial Department of Lands and Forests was also obtained.

"People feel they have a stake in it, so they're committed."
– Member, Mira Pasture Co-op.

"There's nothing does more for a man's initiative than his own potential gains or losses."
– Member, Mira Pasture Co-op.

Untold hours of volunteer time and expertise, by members and other interested community residents, have been the main force behind the development of the pasture. Of the 25 co-op members, all but two are very active. Members have made major inputs of 'sweat equity', contributing many hours of their time, their skills and use of their machinery on a regular basis. This contribution to the physical development of the pasture is in addition to all the hours involved in planning, decision-making, fund-raising, proposal-writing and meeting government officials that the pasture demands.

"We've got a lot of indirect assistance, but mind you, we haven't had any special treatment. We've just finally got the status of a full-time farmer . . ."
– Member, Mira Pasture Co-op.

"Our group – they're real self-starters. They're able to talk to bank managers and negotiate with government – they all have great resources. They're entrepreneurs, problem-solvers. They'll say what they think and be blunt about it . . ."
– Member, Mira Pasture Co-op.

DEVCO and the provincial Department of Agriculture have also provided resources in the form of advice and machinery. Job creation programmes, such as Young Canada Works, Youth Job Corps and Katimavik*, have provided work for young people. These programmes have helped to create the situation whereby land that was forest two years ago has been cleared, stumped, fenced, limed, fertilized and seeded. In the summer of 1979, the first eighty animals were released in the pasture. The plan is to increase the number by 100 animals each year – up to a maximum of 600.

The job creation grants also enabled co-op members to hire a foreman, to supervise and co-ordinate the on-site work. The new foreman/manager was actually not new at all, but a member who had already been working on the pasture as a volunteer. He was able to get a year's leave of absence from his job as a school bus driver.

A barn, 40 feet by 100 feet, has already been constructed on the pasture, in addition to the necessary pens and gates; and a picnic site has been seeded and landscaped. Currently, a log cabin is under construction. It will provide meeting space, and housing for potential caretakers. The plan is to power the cabin with wind, since hydro lines do not reach the pasture.

"We look at everything – every means that there may be a return on . . . We have to generate an income."
– Member, Mira Pasture Co-op.

"The place out there is only limited by your imagination."
– Foreman, Mira Pasture Co-op.

Up until now, selling firewood and gravel obtained from the pasture has provided some cash flow. However, members would like to keep their manager employed on a full-time basis, and therefore need more lucrative sources of income. Everyone – including members – pays a fee for placing animals on the pasture, but this fee is designed only to cover the costs of upkeep. Last year, they initiated an experiment with commercial blueberry production. Hopes are that blueberries will become a major project on the pasture.

"Our blueberry venture holds the key to whether we'll have a success . . . I'm quite confident that we can make a go of that blueberry thing. I think it'll be a great help not just to the pasture itself, but to the community too."
– Foreman, Mira Pasture Co-op.

There are several other plans being considered for the pasture: producing other 'cash' crops, such as Christmas trees or root crops; and, providing a picnic site and recreation area on the pasture. Members of the co-op are justifiably proud of their accomplishment in developing the pasture, and want it to be available to the community at large.

"We're going to get a proper sign. We want to make it a community thing, not just for the members."
– Member, Mira Pasture Co-op.

Anyone can apply to place animals on the field, on a 'first come, first served' basis. Although members of the co-op receive first opportunity to place their animals, they pay the same fees as non-members.

"Interest will rub off a little. People see a farming enterprise that's doing well, they see an area where there's more agricultural activity than there's been for years . . ."
– Member, Mira Pasture Co-op.

Co-op members, in effect, hold the pasture in trust for the community. The charter states that no member may receive any form of direct or special benefit from the co-operative. The great contributions that members have made to the co-op have not been because they hope to sell the improved land at a profit, but rather in order to see a dream come true – and out of a commitment to the preservation of family farming in Cape Breton.

"It's just unfortunate that it wasn't done 50 years ago . . . I think it'll encourage people to go into farming . . . I might still be in dairy, had there been a place like this at the time."

– Member, Mira Pasture Co-op.

What's an Is Five?

The Is Five Foundation is a non-profit corporation. Its offices and conservation store are located in Toronto's Annex area, on the northern edge of the downtown business area; and its recycling centre is situated in the Borough of East York.

"The Is Five Foundation recognizes both a conserver society and a more humane society as essential elements of a sane environment. Our work is a continual development of realistic programmes that include these and other elements. We are not looking for utopia. We are looking for an environment in which we can survive without sacrificing our individual identity. It should allow us to be self-reliant or interdependent to the extent that we choose. Its nature should encourage a more realistic understanding of the value of natural and human resources."
– Promotional flyer, Is Five Foundation.

The '60s and early '70s were a period of social controversy and change in Canada. Many people were advocating a more democratic and humane environment. The roots of the Is Five Foundation are found in the values and ideals of this period. The purpose of the Is Five Foundation is to help in the building of a new society – a 'conserver society'.* However, unlike many groups advocating social change, the members of Is Five stressed the need to move beyond the role of the critic to one of practitioner.

"Our goal is to demonstrate how the ideal can be practiced."
– Member, Is Five.

Toward a Conserver Society:

We are finite beings and we live in a finite world. Natural resources are limited as are the abilities of individuals to appreciate and use resources. Overconsumption, waste and our disposable society not only threaten our finite resources, they discourage appreciation of what we do have while making it ever more difficult to be satisfied with anything. Our convenience economy is running for the convenience of our machinery and the inconvenience of people. We need to become more in touch with the beauty of our world rather than the passive recipients of ever larger quantities of things we cannot even truly be aware of. Physical survival is vital, but virtually meaningless if pursued in isolation. The acceptance and respect for basic human needs convinces us that a more humane society is an equally essential component of a sane environment.
– Promotional flyer, Is Five Foundation.

"We saw recycling as a foot in the door from the beginning. It gave us a credible way to build the conserver society, and a potential for generating revenue."
– Member, Is Five.

In 1974, Is Five was incorporated as a non-profit corporation; and a few months later, received a LIP grant to finance its first community recycling project. The Beaches area of Toronto was chosen as the site. In January 1975, the group began picking up glass and metal. The recycling project was only one part of a larger consumer education effort that included, for example, conservation education programmes in elementary and secondary schools, and workshops on nutrition and organic gardening.

> *"We'd do a school in an area, then cans and bottles would start to appear . . ."*
> – Member, Is Five.

The educational programme was a quiet success. By the end of the LIP period, the cans and bottles set out for collection were exceeding Is Five's 'one truck capacity' to collect them. In areas where homes had received leaflets and schools had been visited to provide information about the programme, participation rates were high: 30 – 40%.

Is Five members felt strongly that the recycling programme was the most productive of its educational efforts and were determined to continue it. The question was how. Already they faced the problems of funding that plague virtually every community economic development effort. Lack of financing during the LIP period had limited their ability to promote the programme throughout the whole collection area. As a result, participation rates were low – too low to generate the revenue needed to lease the second truck that was already badly needed.

The obvious requirement was capital. However, a non-profit community group 'emerging' out of a job creation grant without spectacular evidence of

Is Five began with a single truck, providing a curb-side pick-up of bottles and cans.

being an overwhelming success, does not easily attract investors – Is Five was no exception. The group cut back its programme to cover one-quarter of the original area, worked on a volunteer basis, and contemplated their dilemma. A groundswell of community support strengthened the members' determination to continue, but still did not provide them with an income.

> *"The May-June response from the community was so important. It came literally out of the woodwork – like a breath of life. They sent letters, petitions, telegrams to the city . . . We got a small city grant and bought a half-ton truck and worked for free – with all that support we didn't want to pack it in. We thought: 'We're right. People are saying we're right'. If it had been winter, we might not have thought it was so much fun . . ."*
> – Member, Is Five.

Fall brought a bigger LIP project, spread over much of Metropolitan Toronto. By the following spring, members of Is Five were more than ever convinced that the recycling project was having an educational impact that gave it an importance far beyond the service it provided. It also represented a more effective use of time and resources than seminars and class visits. Using chronically inadequate funding from a variety of sources – LIP, the members themselves, small grants from the city, Canada Works* – Is Five continued its recycling experiment, eventually augmenting its 'sidewalk pick-up' efforts with a depot collection programme.

By late 1976, the recycling experiment could be declared a 'success'. Although no rigorous research had been done, people at Is Five were convinced that the educational impact of the recycling programme was significant – and they also knew that it was a viable business. There was still a problem however – after three years of effort, Is Five members were still without any stable or adequate means of support. The recycling programme was far too small to be able to pay a living wage to the foundation's members.

There followed a year of intensive self-evaluation. Members of Is Five had been convinced for some time that a truly viable recycling project would have to be run on a municipal scale. The combination of skills and knowledge gained during the previous three years, increasing revenues generated from recycled materials, and a growing public recognition of the value of recycling activities, gave Is Five the confidence and clout it needed to approach the Borough of East York. Negotiations began, and in January 1978, a two-year contract – giving Is Five access to paper, cardboard, glass and metal – was signed.

> *"I believe in recycling – we all do. But I also know that there's got to be more to this game than garbage . . ."*
> – Member, Is Five.

At the same time – i.e. in 1977 – members of Is Five had lost their enthusiasm for grants as a source of core funding. To quote: "We realized we were trapped by the opium effect of LIP". Spurred on by a desire to find new sources of revenue and to extend their activities into new areas, members of Is Five struggled through several difficult months.

*"We had to beat back down to what was sustainable, what could have impact, what our **real** focus was . . . You just can't resist continually. You lose your focus. You can't sustain your organization like that. You have to be active, to produce . . . You can't reorganize a community when you don't have a local economic base for yourself."*
– Member, Is Five.

At the end of this soul-searching, Is Five emerged with a new office, a newly incorporated 'for-profit' arm called Resource Integration Systems Limited (R.I.S.), and an ambitious plan involving public relations and resource acquisitions. Very simply, the plan was to move members of Is Five into the consulting field and the printing and publishing business, as a means of breaking out of the 'grants cycle' – and as a way of finding new methods to realize their goals.

"It's kind of amazing that there's all these people getting paid each week. And it feels awfully good to be with a group with these goals, attempting to bring about change . . ."
– Member, Is Five.

"There's a lot of respect for them [*the original members*] *for pulling this thing off . . ."*
– Member, Is Five.

Although there have been many changes in Is Five since 1977, there is still evidence of the original plan in 1980. The East York Recycling Programme – with help from the Economic Growth Component Programme of C.E.I.C.*, the federal Department of Energy, Mines and Resources, and the provincial Ministry of Environment – is now ready to move from 'adolescence' to 'adulthood'. Its financial viability has been established and plans are being developed to 'spin it off' – i.e. to develop a separate organizational structure for it, so that it can operate as a community enterprise, controlled by the people of East York.

Another project which has been 'spun off' is the Recycling Council of Ontario, which was set up to assist groups entering the recycling field. The printing operation, after going through a period of rapid growth, has been deliberately cut back. Members felt that it was too time-consuming and often involved work that was not directly related to their goals. It is currently being restructured – i.e. being integrated more with Is Five's publishing efforts, an activity that is felt to have greater merit as a tool for public education.

This year, Is Five entered the retail business for the first time with a new demonstration project – a conservation store that sells energy-saving consumer goods. After six months of operation, The Conservation Store has been giving every sign of developing into an exciting, viable business, and members of Is Five have already been considering what form its eventual 'spin off' should take.

The consulting business has proven to be a profitable one for members of Is Five, and contracts in the recycling field have helped to cover the bulk of Is Five/RIS's operating costs during the last two years. Is Five's involvement (through one of its members) in Youth Ventures* – a planned community development corporation that will address the needs of unemployed youth in Toronto – has indicated a new direction for their consulting activity to take. In addition to its knowledge and expertise in the recycling field, Is Five's expertise in c.e.d. is now marketable.

Is Five's projects all come under one of two bodies: the Is Five Foundation, a non-profit charitable institution; or R.I.S., a for-profit corporation. Demonstration projects, such as The Conservation Store and East York Recycling, fall under Is Five; 'business' efforts – consulting and printing – fall under Resource Integration Systems Limited. In practice, the division is largely an administrative one. Is Five/R.I.S. has a salary scale, developed by the directors, in consultation with all members. This scale, which attempts to consider need, skill area, level of responsibility and 'market value', defines the limits of financial gain available to employees.

A justifiable concern of everyone at Is Five, is that of internal relationships. The desire to work with people in a mutually supportive environment is as important to the members as any, or all, of their projects combined. Practically everyone in Is Five experiences problems with communication and decision-making. However, these difficulties are overshadowed by the feeling of respect that Is Five members have for each other. In fact, several members describe the group as a 'family'.

> *"When we first started, the idea was to have a humane environment. Even if it's a job like swamping [loading papers onto a truck], everybody should get along. We try to involve everyone in most of the decisions, so everyone feels part of it. We always talk things over."*
> – Member, East York Recycling.

Is Five is not formally organized as a co-operative or a collective. However, the concept of the 'humane working environment', which is the basis for internal relations at Is Five, embodies many principles that are similar to those of co-ops and collectives.

The challenges faced by Is Five demand that members involve themselves in a continuous learning process – i.e. learning by doing.

> *"You are expected to see what needs to be done and how you can fit into it. People don't stop to say: 'Can I do that?'; or, 'Am I trained to do that?' "*
> – Member, Is Five.

These challenges, in turn, encourage the members of Is Five to support each other, which is an important element of their 'humane working environment' concept. New projects and new people are considered to be essential to the ongoing growth and effectiveness of Is Five – as long as they fit into the Is Five's philosophy of a conserver socity and humane working environment.

> *"We have to have new people and new ideas. It gives us life."*
> – Member, Is Five.

"It's a symbiotic relationship. Each staff person that comes into Is Five gives something to the whole and gets something out of it, through the opportunities and skills they pick up."
– Member, Is Five.

This process of giving and receiving is the strength of the Is Five group. Everyone is challenged to give and take as much as they can, which creates a highly energized environment. Is Five, however, is not a group or an idea that everyone could adopt. It's a very demanding working environment, and the people who thrive there tend to be highly motivated, independent, very socially committed and slightly unorthodox.

"I'm more and more interested in how people 'fall off the wheel'. . . I think it tends to be very personal – you meet somebody who has fallen off, and then you fall off. . . After a while it gets easier, then you're no longer part of the mainstream – like this organization. Probably it should not have survived, but it has . . ."
– Member, Is Five.

For Further Reading:

The Centre for Community Economic Development, Washington D.C., publishes a regular newsletter, monographs and books for use by American community development corporations. See page 154 for an address to write to for a list of publications.

Peterson, Rein, **Small Business: building a balanced economy**, Kitchener, Porcepic Press, 1977.

Resource Integration Systems, *A Short History of the Recycling Activities of the Is Five Foundation*, R.I.S., Toronto, 1979.

Science Council of Canada, *Canada as a Conserver Society: resource uncertainties and the need for new technologies*, Report no. 27, Sept., 1977.

Youth Ventures Development Corporation, *Youth Ventures Development Corporation Implementation Proposal 1980-1983*, Social Planning Council of Metropolitan Toronto, 1980.

Getting Started

3

*What does it take to get a community economic development project started? Basically, it requires two things: some thought and some action. Part one of this chapter – **At the Beginning** – discusses some things to think about; Part two – **Forming Your Core Group** – talks about how to move from thought to action.*

At the Beginning – Some Things to Consider

Most community economic development projects begin with a few people sitting around a kitchen table. Regardless of the shape or size of project that develops out of these 'kitchen table' discussions, there are some things to establish at the earliest possible opportunity.

Not every community is ready to begin a non-profit enterprise. The experiences of the communities mentioned in this book indicate that there are seven factors which are significant in terms of your community's ability to successfully organize a community economic development project:

1. A Core Group

> *"What we wanted wasn't just going to happen. We were going to have to get out there and do it."*
> – Member, Mira Pasture Co-op.

Community economic development projects begin when a few people are willing to undertake something new. Often there is nothing unusual about these people; they simply realize that a job only gets done if people do it. These people are your project's first leaders. Their most important quality is their willingness to commit themselves to using economic tools to bring about community development.

2. A Sense of Community

> *"People here have very independent attitudes . . . We have to continually be encouraging them to work together."*
> – Member, Codroy R.D.A.

A community may be geographically based, or it may be based on shared interests or philosophies. When people share a sense of community, they recognize that they have certain common bonds with other members. *The stronger their sense of belonging and the more pride that people take in their membership, the more willing they will be to work together.* For many communities that are considering c.e.d., the first task is to strengthen this sense of commonality and to build the desire to work together. For most communities, this 'task' continues for the life of the project.

3. A Sense of Culture

"Our problems are all partially due to our lack of self-awareness – not knowing our culture . . ."
– Nimpkish Band Member.

A community that is aware of its own history is in a good position to try something new. The development of culture – a sense of the relevance of tradition – is a priority for most community economic development groups.

The Nimpkish People – Culture and Community Development

"This is the land of the potlatch and it was in Alert Bay that the authorities in 1921 arrested Nimpkish people and confiscated their cultural symbols. In spite of this intimidation, the potlatch and the culture have been kept alive by the Nimpkish peoples in Alert Bay."
– *Nimpkish Integrated Development Approach*, 1975, p. 12.

Cultural development has always been an important part of Nimpkish life. Band members feel that an ongoing programme of cultural education is essential, if development efforts are to be successful in Alert Bay. Accordingly, the NIDA plan gives cultural, economic and educational goals equal priority.

"The opening of a centre to house and exhibit the artifacts, to reinforce the cultural pulse of the Nimpkish people and to affect the education of Indian people in the area is critical to the NIDA plan."
– *Nimpkish Integrated Development Approach*, 1975, p. 31.

The development of any community's culture is based on building an awareness of shared past experiences. Cape Bretoners, for example, can speak with pride about their parents' and grandparents' involvement in early efforts at union organizing and establishing co-operatives. Such efforts are part of a long history of finding creative ways to deal with opposition and adversity.

"This emphasis on protecting local communities led many co-operatives of the pre-war years to undertake social or cultural activities . . . In Nova Scotia, most co-operatives had enrichment programs, with the British Canadian in Sydney Mines being particularly devoted to sponsoring varied social activities. In 1908 it began holding annual picnics and, in later years, it funded a town band, a town choir, a theatrical group (which put on some co-operative plays, a few written locally), and a literary society."
– I. MacPherson, *Each for All: A History of the Co-op Movement in English Canada, 1900-1945,* Toronto, 1979, p. 38.

4. Local Leadership

Question: "What makes a good leader?"
Answer: "Biding your time, not getting angry, being articulate and commanding respect."
– Member, Mira Pasture Co-op.

A cultural centre is a critical element of the NIDA plan.

Community history is much more than a good source of tales for winter evenings. The experiences that make history also develop the primary resources needed for any community project: skills and know-how. Most leaders, for example, have been active in at least one community project, and therefore have a lot to offer to subsequent efforts. Different situations call for different leadership responses. Even 'anger' sometimes can be valuable. Often, someone who is a good leader at one stage of a project will not be so helpful at another stage. *Two types of leaders are especially important – the initiator and the manager.*

Initiators: In most communities, there are usually a few people who always get excited about any new project. These people have a lot of initiative and are willing to take risks. Some have previous experience in undertaking new activities; others just realize that if they do not take the first step, no one else will. Once a new project is established, initiators often leave. Since their skills are in 'getting things started', they usually move on to something new. If they do remain with a group, their role will become that of animator – someone who generates enthusiasm and participation.

Managers: Although new ideas, and people with the ability to create them, are essential to an organization in all stages of development, the established project is also dependent upon people who are skilled at the practical aspects of managing and building an organization: running meetings; keeping track of activities; handling money; finding and using resources; developing and maintaining relationships, both internally and externally; and above all, being patient.

Differences in outlook and priorities between managers and initiators often generate conflict. Successful projects have recognized this problem and worked very hard to find ways of using the strengths of both types of leaders.

Is Five's manager/director's description of his working relationship with the organization's initiator/director reflects his appreciation of the way their skills combine: "We temper one another . . . Jack is concerned with process, I'm concerned with results. We have a basic understanding."

5. Community Support

"You've got to change people's attitudes. You've got to get people's commitment before you can do anything. Our plan [NIDA] was adopted by everyone. But people have short memories – some forgot. Now they say that they don't like it. They say, who are we to have all these plans – have our own school, become more independent from Indian Affairs. I say, we're the Nimpkish Band, like it or lump it. If this place is going to get up off its ass, they're going to have to like it. Everyone has to – it's really commitment that matters."
– Member, Nimpkish Band Council.

In situations where a project is well understood and generally approved of, there are many community members who will contribute their skills and knowledge – if they are asked. It seems inevitable that every community project is run by a small group of people, regardless of the size of the total community. It is very important for members of the core group to approach other people and find ways to involve them in the project. Otherwise, the core group can collapse under the strain of being overworked, underskilled and isolated; and what was once a community project, becomes a project of a dwindling core group and no one else.

Although it is not necessary, or feasible, to have total community support, there must be some. *The more support there is, and the more strongly it is expressed, the easier it will be to get your project off the ground.* The acid test of support involves finding out who in your community is willing to commit personal resources – such as money, time, skills or equipment – to a new project.

"My advice is, put a membership fee on the thing and find out how many people have one hundred dollars. See who's committed. . ."
– Member, Mira Pasture Co-op.

If people do not support your project – if they are unwilling to commit themselves to helping out – then your community is not ready to begin a programme of community economic development.

6. Local Resources

"There's always been sheep in the area, and there used to be a mill . . . We've had experience with wool, so we thought it's where we should start. . ."
– Member, Codroy Valley R.D.A.

Most communities have local materials that can be used in the production of marketable goods and services. Rural areas usually have access to 'natural resources' such as land, water, minerals or forests. Urban communities usually have manufactured goods or services that can be linked to community economic development projects. Both rural and urban communities usually have a supply of labour – unemployed or underemployed people, who want to work. Each community has a resource base that gives it both potential and limitations. These have to be identified before a project can be organized.

7. Felt Need

"There seemed to be space for a business like ours. None of the big companies were interested because the market was too small."
– Employee, Comfort Clothing Services.

History tells us that when people feel 'their backs against the wall', they begin to band together. Community economic development projects are often started when some of the local people begin to feel strongly that things have to get better. This force is often what brings people together, and keeps them together during the difficult periods of developing a project.

"Towards the end of the First World War interest in consumer co-operation picked up momentum across Canada. The reasons for this new enthusiasm are clear. Throughout the war there was widespread dissatisfaction over inflation, dissatisfaction embittered by the profiteering exposed in manufacturing industries. The resultant outrage aided co-operators in promoting the consumer movement."
– I. MacPherson, *Each for All: A History of the Co-op Movement in English Canada, 1900-1945,* Toronto, 1979, p. 63.

SUMMARY: Seven Factors to Consider at the Beginning

1. **A Core Group** – a small group of people who are committed to the philosophy of community economic development and who are willing to put in many hours of work.

2. **A Developed Sense of Community** – an understanding of who belongs to the community, what problems and assets members share, and a willingness to work together for mutual benefit.

3. **A Developed Sense of Culture** – a knowledge of local tradition and history, and an awareness of their relevance.

4. **Local Leadership** – people who are willing to take responsibility for starting and managing a project.

5. **Community Support** – people who, although not directly involved in your project, are convinced that it is of value to your community.

6. **Local Resources** – local materials that can be used and have the potential of becoming saleable goods; i.e. of providing a base for a new enterprise.

7. **A Felt Need** – a strong feeling among people in your community that there are issues to be addressed immediately.

Initial kitchen table conversations may not touch on everything contained in the last few pages. However, people who are seriously interested in community economic development have to consider all these factors sooner or later. The general rule is 'the sooner the better'; ignoring them may lead to problems later on. Many communities *are* ready for community economic development – i.e. they have the necessary experience and resources discussed in this section. For these communities, the next question is how to take action . . .

Establishing Your Core Group

You have decided that it's a good time to start a new community-based effort to resolve some local problems. You think that a community economic development project might be the best approach. Your first step in turning your idea into activity is to form a 'core group'.

Finding Your Members

You will need to find some people to work with. In many cases, your initial discussions about whether to begin will have involved only a few people. In order to establish a group capable of organizing a project, your numbers will have to increase. Try to bring together a group of people (six to ten is a good size), who share your concerns and who are willing to do some work. The most important requirement is to have people who can work together.

1. Start Together

Approach each potential member individually. Take the time to explain in detail what has happened up to now, and why you have decided to be part of a community economic development effort. Your group will get off to a much better start, if everyone who joins has the same information and expectations about what will happen.

2. Community Representation

It is also important for your group to be representative of the community. Knowledge of your community can be particularly important. If you know which groups are powerful, which are large and which are most often left out, you can make better decisions about who to approach.

3. Entrepreneurial Spirit

Any community economic development group has to have an 'entrepreneurial spirit' – the ability to see opportunities for money-making ventures, and have the creative energies and business skills to turn these opportunities into successful enterprises. This elusive element can best be captured by attracting people who have expertise in specific areas of business – such as accounting, law or marketing – or who have experience in starting or managing their own business. These people are often just as valuable for their positive attitude towards business, as for the specific skills they offer.

Another potential source of entrepreneurial spirit for your c.e.d. group comes from people who see a direct link between a healthy local economy, and the social and cultural development of their communities. This kind of philosophy was the motivating force behind many of the early co-operatives and credit unions.

For example, early community-organizing efforts in the Maritimes were often undertaken by priests. Today priests and ministers continue to act as sources of 'entrepreneurial spirit' in many parts of the Atlantic Provinces. Priests, with 'running shoes on their feet and hammers in their hands', have been active in organizing the Mira Community Pasture, the Codroy Valley Rural Development Association and other c.e.d. projects not discussed in this book (e.g. 'New Dawn' in Cape Breton).

4. Community Spirit

Every community economic development group needs members who know and understand how community organizations work, and who have a strong interest in social and cultural issues. 'Community spirit' is just as important as 'entrepreneurial spirit'. Not everyone has to have equal interest in both areas, but it is important to try and complement the strengths and weaknesses of fellow members.

> *"I was away for two years, and when I came back, I wasn't too sure about all the changes. I didn't like all this business stuff . . . But I'm really feeling comfortable here now. I really like to come in. I have a lot of respect for what other people are doing."*
> – Member, Is Five Foundation.

The best membership balance happens when your group consists of people who enjoy working with one another, who are representative of your community's various interests, and who are knowledgeable of the workings of business and of the community.

SUMMARY: Establishing Your Core Group

1. Your group should be 'representative'.
2. Everyone joins with the same background information.
3. Include entrepreneurs.
4. Include people who understand how community organizations work.
5. Include people who are interested in the social and cultural needs of the community.
6. Find people who will like working together.

Your First Meeting

When you have formed your group, have a meeting as soon as possible. If people do not know one another, the first item on the agenda should be introductions. The second item should be an explanation of how the meeting has come about. You will need someone to take notes and someone to act as a chairperson, but the formal election of an executive can usually wait. Meanwhile, tasks like chairing, taking notes and keeping track of money can be rotated, or allotted, on a temporary basis.

The best meetings are short, structured and with a set agenda. There is no need to be really formal; just ensure that you keep track of the time so that all items are covered and everyone – especially the shy or quiet people – has an opportunity to talk about why s/he is interested in joining the group.

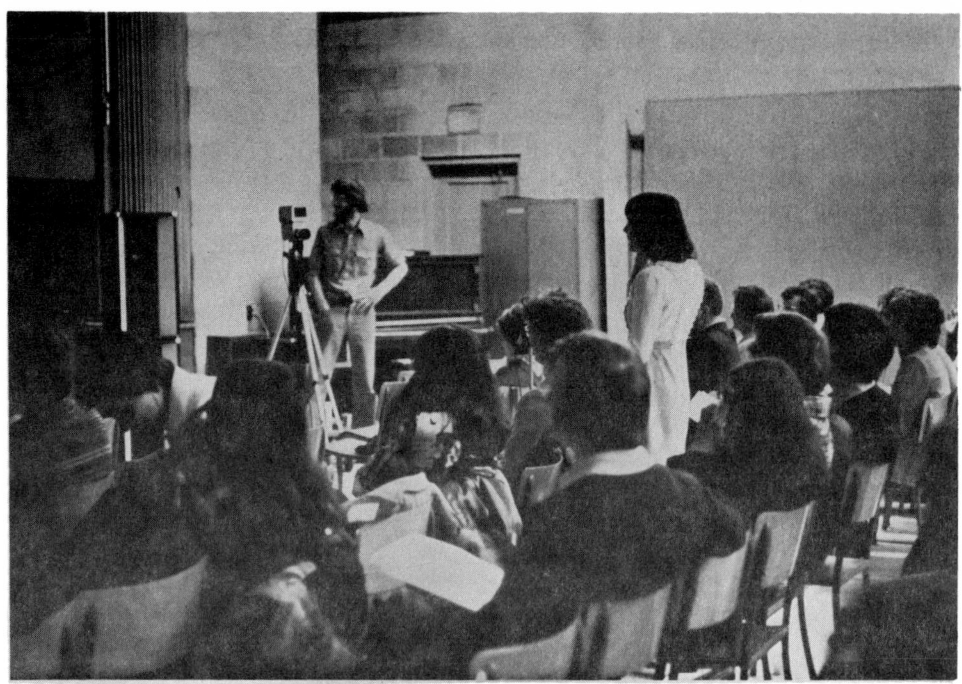

Your first meeting provides an opportunity for people to meet one another and discuss what c.e.d. can mean to the community.

If you have not organized a meeting before, ask someone for advice – or read some of the books and pamphlets written for community groups on how to organize and run meetings. Local libraries, or government departments with responsibilities for social development or recreation, should have this type of information*.

Your first meeting should give people an opportunity to discuss what c.e.d. can mean to your community, and how it might be accomplished. *During the discussion, members of your group will probably find themselves engaged in an argument that will continue for the life of your project. The two sides of the argument are quite simply 'profit' versus 'people'. It should be possible to create a business which is not only profitable, but also humane. However, conditions in our society seem to dictate that tension will always exist between economic and sociocultural priorities. Community economic development groups have found that compromise and collaboration are possible, but not easy to achieve. Your group, over the course of many discussions, will have to find its own way to balance economic, social and cultural priorities equally.*

> *"In practice, the major tension seems to have been between the need for survival of New Dawn as a business enterprise, and its pursuit of social goals. The satisfaction of existing social needs, and the creation of employment, have been the major elements in determining whether or not to enter specific activities . . . Opportunities that appeared promising financially, but served no direct social goal were not pursued, but left to private business . . ."*
>
> – J. Hanratty ed., *New Dawn Enterprises Limited,* Technical Bulletin No. 7, Revised 1979, pp. 52-53.

Try to plan your meeting so that everyone goes away knowing when the next meeting will be, what it will be about, and what needs to be done beforehand. *Move from talk to action as soon as possible.* The ideal situation is for your group to have decided on one or two possible activities by the end of its first meeting.

SUMMARY: Nine Things to Remember at Your First Meeting

1. Have your first meeting as soon as possible.
2. Have an agenda.
3. Have a volunteer chairperson and someone to take notes, but do not elect an executive at this time.
4. Let everyone have a chance to introduce themselves.
5. Explain how the meeting came about.
6. Give everyone an opportunity to discuss their ideas about what community economic development could do for your community.
7. Move to action as soon as possible.
8. Divide up work that needs to be completed before your next meeting.
9. Schedule a time and place for your second meeting, and decide on the items to be discussed.

Your First Activities

The best activities to start with are small and simple: the easiest ones to attempt are social, cultural or recreational – e.g. a public meeting with a guest speaker, a potluck dinner or a baseball game. The only requirement is that they be linked in some way to your group's purpose. Members of your group and people from the rest of the community should be able to see that these activities are merely 'stepping-stones'. *In organizing your first activities, allow for as much community participation as possible, and use only local resources.*

The Mira Community Pasture, for example, began with a series of meetings, held in nearby Sydney at the College of Cape Breton. These meetings led to a feasibility study, which indicated that there was community support for the idea of a pasture. This encouraged the group to continue. However, it was almost three years – and many meetings later – before the Mira Community Pasture Co-operative formally came into existence.

As the Mira Co-op's early history demonstrates, getting started often takes a long time. You will need to be prepared for skepticism and resistance. People can always think of very good reasons why a new idea will not work; just remember that there are equally good reasons why it might. Do not be naive or unrealistic, but do not be too cautious either. According to a Mira Pasture Co-op member: "You just roll up your sleeves and go at it."

For Further Reading:

Connor, Des, **Understanding Your Community**, Oakville, Ontario, Development Press, Second ed., revised 1969.

Doyle, M., Straus, D., **How to Make Meetings Work**, Chicago, Illinois, Playboy Press 1979.

IDERA, *The START Chart: a guide to program development*, Vancouver, International Development Education Research Association, 1978.

MacPherson, Ian, **Each For All: a history of the co-operative movement in English Canada, 1900-1945**, Toronto, MacMillan Ltd., 1979.

4

Planning Your Project

When the first steps are completed – your core group has had some meetings and sponsored a few activities – you are ready to organize your community economic development project. This chapter provides you with an introduction to the process of planning your project. This involves three major steps: developing goals and activities; choosing an organizational structure; and approving and implementing your plan.

Organizing a project usually involves a lot of time spent on planning. It can be tedious work, but well worthwhile in the long run. A plan that is clearly stated can be an invaluable tool for those involved in a project. Your plan is important, not so much for what it says, as for what it does. It provides a common reference point. It is helpful for keeping track of how you are doing, resolving conflicts and making decisions. Your plan is also an excellent way of providing information to outsiders, either to other groups who are interested in what you are doing, or when applying for various forms of assistance.

> *"It is time to create a plan, a process to identify, confront, examine and attack existing and future problems. A mechanism, a developmental model should be built to action alternatives and to involve people in a collective way in tackling the issues and evaluating their efforts. It is a planned overall approach that is needed and in the following pages one will be proposed."*
> – *Nimpkish Integrated Development Approach,* 1975, p. 13.

> *"Early on, we prepared a brief – put our ideas down on paper. Essentially they haven't changed. The process of developing the brief was good. It made it clearer what people wanted to do. We had lots of discussions before we wrote the brief . . . what developed out of our discussions . . . gave our group some sort of ideology. It's been a kind of guiding light."*
> – Member, Mira Pasture Co-op.

Your plan does not have to be long or complex, although it can be – e.g. the NIDA plan. The length and type of your plan will depend mostly on how your group operates. All groups have to plan; those that do it well will commit considerable time and effort to their planning, and put the results together in written form. On the other hand, it is important not to spend too much time on planning. *After all, a group's success will be helped by its plan, but it will be judged by its actions.*

> *"Take the planning lightly . . . and spend your every minute hustling to do what's got to be done. Use every minute gainfully. Get up and get at it, and the plan looks after itself."*
>
> – Member, Mira Pasture Co-op.

There will always be some people in your group who are impatient with the time that planning takes. Others may want to spend an indefinite period of time at it. Try to find a middle road. Many groups solve this problem by appointing a special committee to do the background work – e.g. CCEC.

Groups develop their plans in various ways. It is not uncommon for a community group to operate for two or three years before it gets around to putting a plan on paper. Is Five is an example of such a group. Other groups make developing a plan the focus of their activities right from the beginning, spending many months on developing a complex and detailed document – e.g. Contact and NIDA. In some cases, groups wait until a need arises – usually for money or technical help – before putting anything down on paper.

It is important to recognize that planning has to take place. It should be as public a process as possible. It should be done only to the extent that it is useful as a guide for decision-making and potential activity. You should be prepared to review and change your plan often, as you learn from your mistakes and from your successes. No plan is perfect, but every good plan is helpful.

The acquisition of the old school made the realization of NIDA's educational goals possible.

STEP 1: Developing Goals and Activities

Planning involves two initial steps: determining what you hope to achieve – i.e. your goals; and deciding what you are going to do to attain these goals – i.e. your activities. *Identifying community needs* is the starting point, followed by a *search for local resources.* By *matching* community needs with available resources, you will be able to identify appropriate goals and activities for your group. You should also take into account individual preferences; it is always best to organize your priorities around the skills and interests of your group members, when trying to get a project off the ground.

1. Identifying Community Needs

"A good fishing season helps everybody. This is a fishing town . . . The future of fishing here? I don't know. It's been not too good the last two years and it'll be worse for the next three. We used to have the biggest fleet of fishing boats around in the late '60s. It's declined now to fifteen boats. Last year there must have been 150 kids wandering the streets. There's nothing else to do here. And there's another 200 to 300 kids who are seven, eight or nine years old now . . . We're always trying to find a way to create employment."
– Member, Nimpkish Band Council.

The plan that will guide your group's activities must be based on what members of the community feel needs to be done. Community economic development projects require a strong commitment. When people know that your project is locally relevant, they are more likely to provide the necessary support.

The best way to start is by asking your own group members what they think is important. Sometimes community economic development groups are organized around one particular identified 'need'. Comfort Clothing, for example, arose out of a perceived need to provide jobs for female single parents. Other times, the concern that brings a group together may be more general – i.e. the 'something-has-got-to-be-done-around-here-and-nobody-is-going-to-do-it-unless-we-do' type. *In general, it is necessary to identify what has 'got to be done', and then establish which items on the list should be attacked first.*

Find out who agrees with your group's assessment of 'need', and what other community members think is important, by:

a) conducting a telephone survey;

b) conducting a survey through the mail;

c) placing an article in the local newspaper and asking for responses;

d) hosting a potluck dinner and having people discuss community needs; or,

e) hosting a formal community meeting to discuss local problems.

The approach your group uses should be fair, in that it gives interested people a chance to participate. Solicit opinions from as wide a variety of people as possible – include skeptics as well as sympathizers.

"During our first three months, we were real outsiders. No community leaders were involved in our recycling project. But then we reached a real watershed. I think the breakthrough came with the ***Ward Nine News*** *[a community newspaper] – they wrote about us. Volunteers started coming in. And we started to produce a regular newsletter. All this positive feedback started coming in – not orchestrated at all . . ."*
– Member, Is Five.

Needs Identification will help you to*:

1. *Understand your community's problems:* what should be attacked first; which problems should get more attention than others; and which problems can be left safely on the 'back burner'.

2. *Understand the people in your community:* what do local people feel is important; what do local people feel is feasible; what are local people willing to do for themselves; and what are some of the local resources.

3. *Identify areas of support:* who is willing to help out; under what conditions can you expect assistance; who will not help; and what reason is given – e.g. lack of interest – for this unwillingness.

2. Searching for Local Resources

In order to develop ideas for goals and activities, you also need to know what local resources are available. Since the search for resources is such an important and complex part of successful community economic development projects, we have devoted a whole chapter to it [see Chapter 5].

It is open to question whether you should determine goals and activities and then look for resources, or whether you should first determine what is available and then plan activities around what you find. Books on project planning – like this one – will recommend that the first step should be to determine available resources. In practice, however, many groups think about what they would like to do first, then start looking around for the tools to do it with. The important thing is that the two – resources and activity planning – go together. *Do not plan goals and activities without considering how you are going to make them happen. Do not embark on a lengthy investigation of available resources until you have some idea of how you want to use them.*

3. Matching Needs and Resources

In order to plan, your group must know the 'needs' – i.e. problems that people in your community feel are important and require attention – its community economic development project should address. It should also be aware of which local resources have the potential to provide a good base for profit-generating activities. It is a good idea to list and describe the needs and resources you have identified; remember to note where your information has come from. Your guide to selection of project goals and activities lies in the matching of community needs and locally available resources.

A SAMPLE . . .

Community Needs	Information Sources	Local Resources	Information Sources
• reduce unemployment • increase availability of local goods and services	• Manpower statistics • local employers • local priest • community survey	• available farmland • local interest in raising sheep • historical involvement with wool industry (i.e. expertise) • available labour	• Dept. of Agriculture • Manpower statistics • Dept. of Rural Development • community survey

Project Goals:
- To provide local jobs.
- To manufacture a product that will be used locally.

Project Activity:
- Woollen mill†

---

4. Generating Ideas for Goals and Activities

By the time your working group has examined community needs and resources, and has spent several meetings talking about why it is together, your objectives will probably be quite clear. However, if this is not the case, *try brainstorming**. Take the time to list everyone's ideas about what might happen; do not discuss them. Once you have a long and interesting list, group the ideas into categories. Then begin to weed through them, discarding the totally unacceptable ones. Separate the goals (such as jobs), from the activities (such as an auto body shop). Hopefully, for each goal, you will have several activities to choose from.

Goals: Your goals should build on what already exists – i.e. the history of your community, its needs and resources. Your goals should be ambitious but not grandiose. Try to concentrate on the impact you would like your project to have – the contents rather than the packaging. For example, if your community needs jobs, creating permanent work for community residents should be your goal. In your list of possible activities, there could be: creating a community development corporation; finding a good franchise to introduce; or attracting new industry.

† Although the sample is hypothetical, it is based on the story of the Codroy Valley Rural Development Association.

ANOTHER SAMPLE . . .

Community Need	Information Sources	Local Resources	Information Sources
• jobs for single parents with little or no previous work experience	• statistics from Manpower and Social Services • participants in educational upgrading programme	• unskilled labour force • on major transport route; close to urban markets • expertise in fashion design	• Manpower statistics • community survey • Chamber of Commerce • Industrial development officer • Federal Business Development Bank • local community college

Project Goals:

- To provide permanent employment for single parents.
- To provide training for unskilled workers.
- To establish a worker-owned manufacturing business.

Project Activity:

- Small garment industry, producing specialty clothes for an identified market†

Have both short-term and long-term goals. Think about what you would like to see happen ten years from now: your ideas about what the future could look like will be your long-term goals. Think about what you would like to see in five years time; then in two. Your plan for two years ahead should be checked for practicality. Is it really possible for your organization to accomplish all that in two years? Often groups are overly optimistic at first, and then become discouraged because they are not progressing quickly enough. They never stop to realize how unrealistic their first plans were. Short-term goals are usually easier to identify. They are the results you would like to see as soon as possible – i.e. within eight to twelve months. Some groups prefer to start with the immediate future and leave worrying about the long-term goals until later. This is fine, as long as it is not left too late.

Your discussions should concentrate on the positive aspects, rather than on all the potential difficulties. Your group will have plenty of time to consider barriers and problems later on. At this stage, it is the time for optimistic thinking. What is important is that everyone shares an understanding of why your group is doing what it intends to do – i.e. its goals and philosophy.

> *"I work here because we all share a philosophy, a responsibility to attain our goals . . . Everyone here is an 'Is Five person' – each person brings skills which are added to the whole and everyone gets something out of it, by the opportunity and the skills they pick up . . . But it's the philosophy that makes it a whole, because the people keep coming and going."*
>
> – Member, Is Five Foundation.

† This sample is also hypothetical, but based on the story of Comfort Clothing Services in Kingston.

Activities: When your core group has established its goal(s), take a look at the suggestions for activities. Do they fit your goals? Refer back to your information on local needs and resources. Which activities not only respond to identified needs, but also can be supported by local resources?

ANOTHER SAMPLE . . .

Community Need	Information Sources	Local Resources	Information Sources
• support for local agriculture	• local agriculture rep. • community survey • County Council	• available farmland • expertise in farming • useable wood for fences and buildings • loaned machinery (e.g. tractors)	• local opinion • Dept. of Agriculture • local farming population • community survey

Project Goal:
- To support part-time farmers by increasing the amount of available pasture land.

Project Activity:
- Co-operative community pasture†

If you have ideas for activities that seem to be consistent with community needs, local resources and your identified goals, check them out against the following criteria:

1. Which activities respond to needs that are considered high priority in your community?
2. Which activities use local resources that are inexpensive and easily accessible?
3. Which activities are more labour intensive, as opposed to capital intensive?
4. Which activities will be simple to start up and to manage?
5. Which activities involve tasks and ideas that are familiar?
6. Which activities are members of your core group most interested in working on?

The activity that rates the highest will be your best starting point.

If you do not have any ideas for activities, or if your ideas do not fit in with your goals, needs and resources, your next step is to review your efforts to date. What have you missed or ignored? It is unusual for a community not to be able to match these elements. However, if your group cannot reach agreement on which activity is best to start with, you may want to call in outside help. Sometimes, other community organizations or local educational

† This sample is also hypothetical, but based on the story of the Mira Community Pasture Co-operative.

institutions will help you to assess your situation for a low fee, or in return for payment of expenses.

Sheep raising has always been important to the people of the Codroy Valley.

"The idea [for the mill] came up in 1976. We had turned the Sports Complex over to the Sports Committee to run and we wanted a new project. We wanted to do something about employment here . . . The idea for the mill came up because the valley was known as a mill area. We had two mills here in the 1940s . . . We hoped it [the mill] would help to revive sheep farming. It's really gone down around here. There's only 8,000 breeding ewes left in Newfoundland now. People from Quebec and St. Pierre have been buying them . . ."
– Member, Codroy R.D.A.

"We knew there was a good local market. Lots of people knit their clothes here still. We had a lot of experience in that area [working with wool] . . ."
– Member, Codroy R.D.A.

The members of the Rural Development Association took these ideas and explored the possibility of establishing a small woollen mill. In association with the Newfoundland Department of Agriculture and DREE, they explored sources of wool, potential markets, potential employees, community support and transportation services. Discussions were held in the local community, government statistics were assessed, and numerous meetings of board members and government officials were held to examine the financing of the project.

Many community economic development groups break down their goals and activities according to whether they are social, economic or cultural. This is one good way to make sure that you have given sufficient priority to all three areas. It is important to remember, though, that the essence of c.e.d. lies in developing a relationship between the three. Therefore, if you have difficulty deciding which category certain goals or activities come under, it is a good sign rather than a bad one.

STEP 2: Choosing a structure

In order to reach your goals, your organization will need to be 'structured' in some way. Ideally, the structure you choose will be one that allows you to organize and manage your activities with minimum wasted effort and maximum impact. The decision you make about the appropriate structure for your organization is an important one. The structure you choose will have a significant impact on the social, legal and financial elements of your work.

The structure of your organization must reflect your philosophy. It must also be appropriate to your particular activities – both profit and non-profit – and to your community. Your organizational structure should take into account the history of your community, the skills of your own group, and the changes that the future can be expected to bring.

The challenge for c.e.d. groups is to develop a structure that is:
a) *functional*, in that it promotes efficient and effective work;
b) *flexible*, so that it can roll with the (usually) frequent punches;
c) *open*, so that it allows for as much distribution of responsibility and as much active participation in decision-making as possible; and,
d) *understandable*, so that people will not feel threatened or disturbed by it.

The ideal structure does not exist. Community economic development organizations are constantly adjusting their structures to the trade-offs that seem to be necessary. For example, the more 'open' an organization is, the longer it generally takes to make decisions, and as a result, the less 'functional' it is. A similar trade-off often exists between the 'flexible' and 'understandable' factors.

A good structure in one situation is not good in another. For example, different communities across the country have had varying experiences with co-ops. Some communities now welcome and appreciate co-ops; others see them as a good way to lose a lot of money. Therefore, as a rule of thumb, where historical experience with co-ops has not been good, the co-op structure should usually not be used. After all, the co-op structure is not the only form suited to community economic development. In fact, the 'community business' and the 'community development corporation' are probably more common. Each one has its advantages and disadvantages. Groups often move naturally from one structure to another, as they grow and develop.

> *"In 1976, there was a major expansion and change in the organization. Members concluded that the co-op structure did not fully suit the wide-ranging activities of the group, as well as its need for flexibility . . .*

Thus, in June 1976, members formed a new organization called New Dawn Enterprises, and it was incorporated as a non-profit company. . ."
– J. Hanratty ed., *New Dawn Enterprises Limited*, technical Bulletin No. 7, Revised 1979, p. 3.

1. Types of Organizations

The Community Business: The community business is the simplest of the community economic development structures. It is used when groups have, as the main focus of their activities, a single enterprise that has been chosen both for its profit-making potential and for the social benefits it provides. A community business is non-profit and community-owned, with a voluntary board of directors. It is generally started in order to create jobs and/or to provide a needed service or product locally. Sometimes, as at Comfort Clothing, a few of the directors are also employees. Those employees who sit on the board do so voluntarily and receive no extra financial benefits – although lately, some thought has been given to paying expenses, such as baby-sitting costs.

Many community economic development groups start with a community business, then move to a community development corporation type of structure as they add activities.

COMMUNITY BUSINESS: COMFORT CLOTHING SERVICES

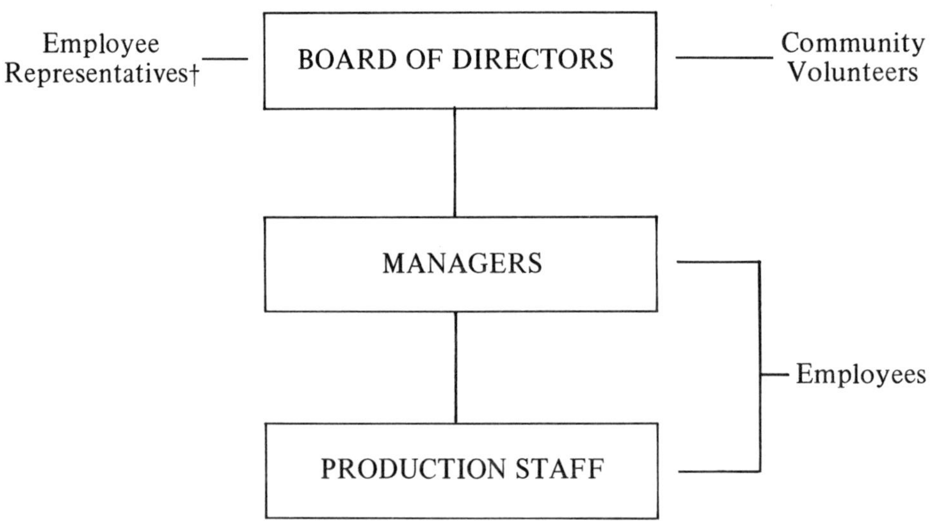

† Majority of Board members are employees.

The Co-operative: Like community businesses, co-ops are started in order to provide a needed service or to generate employment. The co-op structure is used in many situations. In order to join a co-op, a prospective member must purchase one or more shares of a limited total. Most co-ops limit the number of shares any one member or family can hold, in order to ensure that the number of members does not eventually diminish to just a few. Co-ops also stipulate that each member has only one vote, no matter how many shares he or she may own, in order to ensure that control of the organization is widely distributed.

The members of the co-op are the owners. They elect an executive to oversee the co-op on their behalf. The difference between a traditional co-op and a c.e.d. co-op is that in the case of the former, the co-op is run for the benefit of its members, while the latter is run for the whole community. Co-op members act, in effect, like a board of directors, operating on behalf of their community.

What a Community Economic Development Co-op Looks Like

1. All members own a limited number of shares.
2. Each member has one vote, no matter how many shares s/he may own.
3. The members of the co-op elect an executive to represent them.
4. The executive consists of elected members.
5. All major decisions are discussed and voted on by the members.
6. Community economic development co-ops, unlike traditional co-ops, are as concerned about community needs as they are about membership needs.

Credit unions are co-ops. CCEC is both a credit union and a c.e.d. organization. Co-ops may be small, like Mira Pasture, which has twenty-five members; or they may be large, like JAL in Quebec – a large central co-op with many members and several enterprises operating under its 'umbrella'.*

In most cases, not only are co-op members owners and directors or officers, but they also hold any paid staff positions. This often evolves naturally. Many co-ops begin – e.g. CCEC and Mira Pasture – with no paid staff. All work is done by volunteers. As the organization grows and increases its revenues, it begins to pay these 'volunteers'. This is exactly what happened at the Mira Pasture Co-op.

CO-OPERATIVE: MIRA COMMUNITY PASTURE

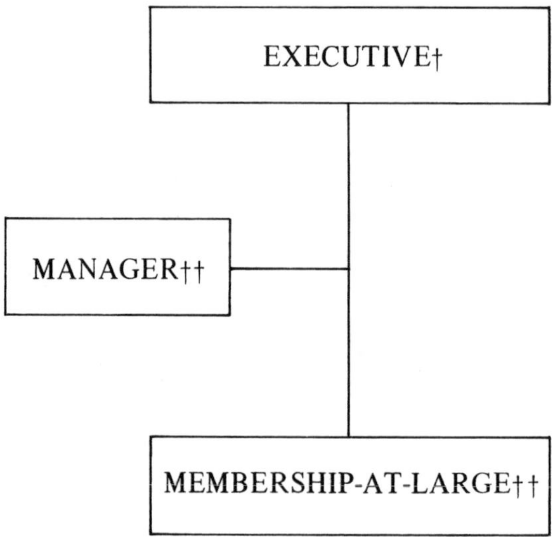

† Members of the co-op, elected by members-at-large.

†† An employee of the co-op; not necessarily a member.

††† Twenty-five share-holding members, each with one vote.

Community Development Corporations: This name is one we have recently borrowed from the United States, but the structure itself has been in existence in Canada for many years. A community development corporation is an umbrella organization. It co-ordinates and directs a variety of not-for-profit developmental activities.

In some ways, it acts like any corporation. It provides services to its 'branch' projects, like secretarial and bookkeeping assistance, that would otherwise have to be duplicated. It can also transfer necessary resources – e.g. people and money – from one activity to another. In this way, profits from a well-established enterprise can be used to subsidize other ventures.

This structure can be used, not only as a base from which to initiate activities, but also to perform a partnership function for other businesses; for example, by providing capital in exchange for equity – i.e. partial ownership. In this way, it can also operate as a kind of local venture capital corporation.

Community development corporations are started by groups who want to initiate a variety of projects. In contrast to community businesses and most co-ops – where one activity is a means for achieving social, economic and cultural goals all at once – community development corporations will often identify separate not-for-profit 'activities' in each 'goal' area.

COMMUNITY DEVELOPMENT CORPORATION: CONTACT

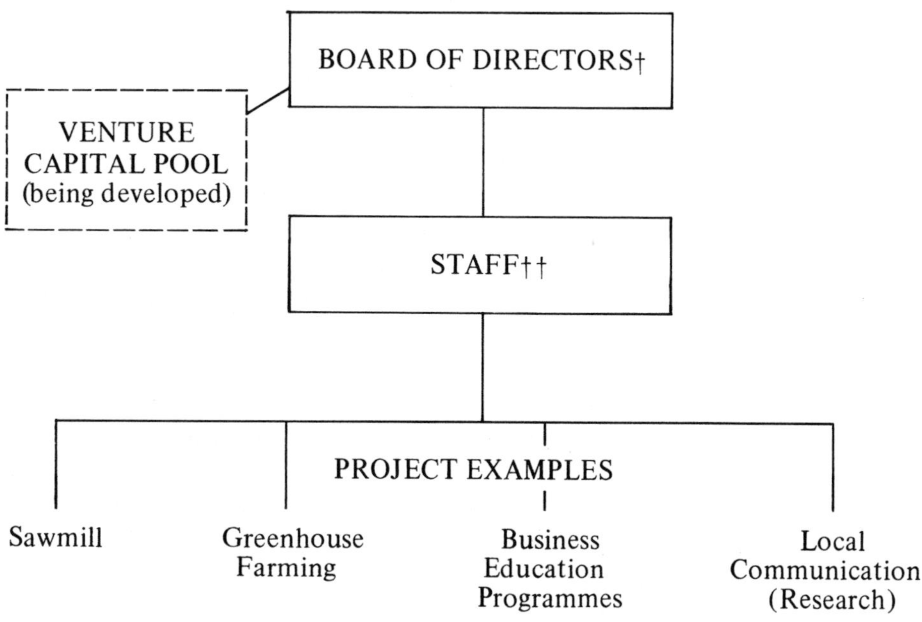

† 15 residents, representing various regions and interest groups.

†† Co-ordinator, secretary, information officer, technical resource people (agriculture, forestry, economics).

Other Structures: These are the most common structures. There are others that are hybrids of the ones described in this section. For example, Is Five operates like a community development corporation, except for the fact that its board members are all staff members. As with a co-op, members of Is Five run their organization 'in trust' for the larger community they serve. Community members participate in Is Five operations through participation in projects – such as East York Recycling – or through working as volunteers, rather than through direct representation on the board of directors.

There are also other less common structures, such as c.e.d. networks. As with co-ops, network members contribute a percentage of their savings and time to the development of not-for-profit projects. However, they do not formalize themselves until after the project is well underway. They then incorporate the project as a non-profit venture, and elect or appoint a board of directors. The sponsoring group itself remains informal, reviving itself on an ad hoc basis, if and when necessary. The 'network' structure is good for temporary situations, but its informality tends to leave too much to chance. Community economic development groups may start out with a network structure, but they usually move on to a more stable organizational arrangement after a short period of time.

2. Incorporating and Other Legal Matters

Groups incorporate for a number of reasons, but there are three primary ones.

Limited Liability:

One is limited liability. If a group is incorporated, and someone sues it or the group goes bankrupt, the creditors can take as payment only what the group itself owns or has rights to. Creditors cannot seize the personal property of group members as payment. Therefore, each group member has limited liability – the amount of money or property that s/he can lose is limited to whatever has been invested in, or pledged, the group. If a group is not incorporated, individual members can be held liable for any or all of the group's debts.

Finances:

The second reason is financial. Groups which are non-profit are eligible to become charities, and can then give tax receipts for donations. Groups that are profit-oriented are eligible for certain tax advantages. Any registered business – incorporated or not – can 'write off' certain business expenses at tax time.

Legitimacy:

The third reason has to do with legitimacy and credibility. Many c.e.d. organizations incorporate: as non-profit corporations, in order to distinquish themselves from 'regular' businesses and corporations; as 'for-profit' corporations, in order to distinguish themselves from 'charities'; or as both, in order to be able to use either 'identity' as needed.

Community economic development organizations usually decide to incorporate so that they have limited liability and legitimacy. The financial advantages are not usually significant enough to warrant incorporation during the first few years. The exception to this is that eligibility for grants from governments or foundations sometimes requires groups to be incorporated as non-profit corporations.

When your group begins to think about incorporating, consider these additional points:

a) incorporation is time-consuming;
b) you will need a lawyer's help;
c) you will need an accountant's advice if you are incorporating 'for-profit';
d) incorporation costs money ('for-profit' incorporation costs up to $1,000);
e) new groups can often affiliate themselves with already incorporated groups as a committee or project, and delay incorporating, although only for a limited time;
f) incorporation is much easier if you can find a 'model' (a charter of an already incorporated group that has purposes and activities similar to yours); and,
g) you will need a board of directors, an executive, a registered name and a list of 'objectives' for your organization.

3. How to Incorporate

How to incorporate varies from province to province. Most c.e.d. groups incorporate provincially, although those that expect to do business in more than one province or country sometimes incorporate federally. In general, the choices are as follows:

Not to Incorporate:

You can register your profit-generating activities as one of two types of businesses: sole proprietorship (one owner), or a partnership (two or more owners). Community economic development organizations usually register their activities as partnerships, because they always involve more than one owner. Partnerships may be general or limited. General partnerships mean that all partners are managers and investors, and therefore share equal responsibility. Limited partnerships include some people who are investors only. 'Silent partners' are not actively involved in the business and do not assume all the debts of the business. Only the active members of the partnership can be held personally liable.

There are several advantages to registering your enterprise as a partnership: it is simple, inexpensive and yet still makes you an 'official' business. The disadvantages are: except where limited partnerships are available, liability is unlimited; and your eligibility for some forms of financing may be affected.

To Incorporate as a Non-profit 'Society':

Regulations for non-profit corporations vary from province to province. In some provinces, non-profit corporations cannot carry on business, making it impossible for c.e.d. groups to use this structure. In others, non-profit organizations can carry on business as long as their purpose is not just to run enterprises. Non-profit corporations are also known as 'societies' or 'corporations without share capital'.

It is quite common for c.e.d. groups to start off with a 'non-profit' status, either by incorporating themselves or by operating as part of another established non-profit corporation. It gives them the advantages of limited liability, legitimacy with funding groups, and eligibility to apply for a charitable number, if they want one. Registration is usually inexpensive. Most groups can find a 'model' to use in drawing up their papers; this is always less expensive than having a lawyer do all the work. Just make sure you have a lawyer check the results. The disadvantages to this structure are the legal limitations on the amount of business your organization can do, and the fact that most people – including bank managers – cannot accept that a non-profit organization is also a business organization.

To Incorporate as a 'For-profit' Corporation:

You can incorporate as a limited company – i.e. a corporation with share capital. This legal structure was designed for companies: that sell shares to shareholders; who elect or appoint a board of directors; which in turn hires a president; who then manages the organization. Profits often are retained for reinvestment in the business, but the basic rationale is that profits will be distributed to shareholders.

The incentive to buy shares is based on the expectations that the value of the shares will rise with the value of the company, and that dividends will be paid to shareholders. The more shares you hold, the more influence you have, because your percentage of ownership is greater.

Limited companies may be private or public. Public companies sell shares on the open market and are usually very big. Community economic development organizations in Canada are unlikely ever to go 'public'; they, like most Canadian companies, will remain private corporations.

Community economic development organizations that incorporate as limited companies inevitably have to 'bend' the structure to suit their philosophy and purposes. How your group does this will depend on your respective provincial or federal regulations. Many groups do things like: incorporate, but never distribute shares; or sell shares for a nominal price to all community members. They also add clauses specifying that the directors and/or owners cannot gain personally from the profits of the corporation; or they set up a system whereby the right to collect dividends is waived. The advice of a sympathetic lawyer is very important if you make 'adjustments' to this structure.

The advantages of 'for-profit' incorporation are: limited liability, combined with legitimacy as a business; the right to carry on business; and the tax allowances available to you. There are several disadvantages. You will be using a legal structure designed for other purposes, so incorporation will be complicated and time-consuming. A lawyer will probably have to do most of the work for you, which will be expensive – not to mention the cost of the registration fee. Your accountant should also be consulted; this will mean another expense. In addition, some people will assume that social goals are no longer important – that you just want to make money.

Incorporate Twice – Once as Non-profit/ Once as For-profit:

This is neither illegal nor crazy. It is sometimes the best solution for groups that want to be able to walk into the bank and talk with their manager on the same terms as any other business, yet still be clearly non-profit. Is Five is an example of a group that has chosen this route. Groups that incorporate twice have overlapping or identical boards of directors, and usually, identical staff. Projects are officially divided up – some belong to the non-profit corporation and some to the 'for-profit' corporation. Other groups incorporate their central organization in one form, then incorporate projects

The East York Recycling Programme is a 'spin-off' from the Is Five Foundation and has its own independent structure.

separately as they mature. Often this is in preparation for 'spinning off' – i.e. giving a former project its own independent structure (e.g. East York Recycling).

Co-operatives: Every province has different co-op legislation. Co-ops wear a variety of legal 'hats', depending on their size and location. Your credit union or other local co-operatives are often your best sources of information. In provinces like Saskatchewan, Nova Scotia and Quebec, where co-operatives are important historically and economically, there are provincial departments with special responsibilities for co-operative development. These departments have field officers and written information to help you decide how to proceed.

SUMMARY: Advantages and Disadvantages of Different Corporate Firms

	Advantages	Disadvantages
1. No Incorporation (sole proprietorship/partnership)	• simple to do • inexpensive • legitimacy • owner(s) in direct control	• restricted access to some forms of financing • unlimited liability, unless you are a limited partnership
2. Non-profit Society (corporation without share capital)	• simple to do • inexpensive • owner(s) in direct control	• not viewed as legitimate form for business
3. For-profit Corporation (corporation with share capital)	• limited liability • legitimacy • tax allowances	• expensive • can be complicated (e.g. closely regulated, extensive recordkeeping necessary)
4. Co-operatives	• shareholders in direct control • pooled resources of members give organization greater financial strength	• in some areas not viewed as 'credible' form of business • often difficult to keep members active

4. How to Proceed with Incorporation

Gather Information: When your group starts to think about incorporating, your first job will be to gather information. Write away to the appropriate provincial department – e.g. industry or commerce – for information. Talk to other groups about how they incorporated. Books are available, the complexity of which vary.

Consult a Lawyer: You will probably need to find a lawyer to advise you on an appropriate legal structure. If your group does not know any lawyers personally, try contacting your community legal aid clinic – if you have one. The people there will probably not handle your work themselves, since most clinics concentrate on personal legal matters. Some clinics, however, do work with community groups; or they can often recommend a lawyer who is likely to understand your needs. The other route is to approach a legal firm. Some firms are able to spread their work around so that they can 'donate' time to worthy local causes at reduced prices.

In looking for a lawyer, there are certain things to be aware of. One is that law schools teach their students virtually nothing about co-operatives or other forms of not-for-profit enterprises. Even those who specialize in business or corporate law will have little background in the work you are asking them to do. There are some lawyers who have a special interest in 'community' law or 'co-op' law, but they learn about it on their own. Since there is no established body of knowledge, you are likely to get conflicting advice from different lawyers. In general, if you find a lawyer who is genuinely interested in working with your group, count yourself lucky.

The other thing is that you should expect to pay for good legal advice. A lawyer's time is expensive. For a non-profit group, sympathetic lawyers will often reduce their fees or do some work for free. This decision, however, rests with the lawyer. You are far better off paying for good legal advice, than to receive an off-the-cuff opinion for free.

Consult an Accountant: Consult with your accountant before incorporating. *Within the first year after your organization starts a profit-making enterprise, you will need the services of an accountant. The best approach is not to wait until audit time, but to consult an accountant as soon as you begin business.* Advice can be given about how to set up your books and organize the finances of your business. Keep the same things in mind when hiring an accountant as applied when finding a lawyer: nothing in your accountant's formal training prepares him/her for c.e.d. work, so expect mistakes in the beginning; and expect to pay for your accountant's time.

With both lawyers and accountants, try to stay with the same people, unless you find evidence of incompetence or corruption. The more your lawyer or accountant knows about you, the better s/he can advise you.

Register Your Name: Your next step will be to register the name of your organization. In some cases, you will have to pay for this. Your provincial or federal government office will give you the necessary forms to fill out.

Prepare Incorporation Papers: While your name is being registered, you can begin working on your incorporation papers. They come with instructions, but you will probably also need the help of books, other 'models' and your lawyer.

Hold an Annual Meeting: After your papers have been filed and returned to you, your organization will be required to hold a general meeting within a specified time (three months to one year), to ratify your constitution and bylaws, as described in your articles of incorporation.

5. Other Legal Considerations

There are additional legalities involved in starting a business. Depending upon the type of enterprise you choose, you may need to get licences or permits. Check out zoning regulations, building standards, labour regulations, taxes (such as municipal business, provincial sales and federal income taxes), unemployment insurance regulations and other insurance needs. Your lawyer, your accountant and your local Chamber of Commerce – if you have one – can help to sort out which regulations affect you.

STEP 3: Approving and Implementing Your Plan

1. Approval

When you are putting together your plan, make sure that you have included the ideas of as many people as possible – both from inside and outside your group. Make an effort to incorporate ideas that people in your community like and understand.

> *"You can't run too far ahead – you will only cause alienation. You must believe that people want a good world, that they are willing to change and want to participate in making changes happen – if they understand."*
> – Member, Is Five Foundation.

Once your group has made its choices regarding goals, activities and structure, you should put together a 'first draft' of your plan and take it to other members of the community. Use local media, public meetings, consultations with local organizations, surveys or any other means available to you. Arrange to discuss your ideas informally with a number of people in your community who are generally well-respected. Make sure you ask them to talk to other people who they think might be interested in what you are hoping to do. Check back with these people in a couple of weeks to find out their reactions to your ideas.

> *"In early fall, a document synthesizing the recent experiences of communities and the philosophies which inspired these experiences was published and made available free of charge to all the people of the area. It was entitled "Communiqu' Action" . . . In the spring of '77 the general plan of the project was made public to the people and organizations of each of the communities in question as well as the regional community intervention organizations . . . After pledging their support to the project in principle, several organizations made various recommendations which more accurately assessed the needs and more clearly identified the structure . . . This approach moreover helped to establish clearly the complementary roles to be played between existing structures (without competition) and the Pilot Project . . ."*
> – Le Groupe Contact, Projet Contact, 1977, pp. 13-14 .

2. Commitment

When your plan has been inspected and your group has made relevant changes, your plan should be formally ratified. In fact, this is the point at which many groups formalize themselves. They incorporate and/or elect an executive, so that they can hold a formal vote. It is very important not to rush through this last task. Make sure that any reservations members of your group have about the plan have been brought out into the open and discussed. Amend the plan if necessary. The most important thing is to have a product that people will like and are willing to work on.

After your plan has been ratified by your group, take it to your community for discussion and approval. You are highly unlikely to get total support, but if people have been consulted along the way, and if the plan truly addresses community needs, many people will support it.

3. Implementing Your Plan

Now that you have a plan, it's time to get working on it. Try to arrange it so that within the first few months after your plan has been ratified, your group has more than one activity started. That way, if one activity fails, your group will have others to fall back on. At the same time, however, do not overload yourselves. Start things one at a time.

Discuss each project activity carefully. Keep good notes about what tasks need to be done to get an activity started, who has agreed to work on them, and when the tasks will be completed. Make progress reports a regular part of each meeting. Work on activities in small groups, so that you can give each other support on a daily basis.

Do not rush. Many community economic development groups feel pressure to justify themselves to their own communities, and therefore undertake activities too quickly. Remember that c.e.d. projects go on for five, ten, twenty years and more. Your organization will have plenty of time to prove itself to the community.

For Further Reading:

Knowles, Malcolm, **The Modern Practice of Adult Education: andragogy vs. pedagogy**, New York, Association Press, 1970.

Ministry of Consumer and Commercial Relations (Ontario), *The Incorporator's Handbook*, Toronto, 1979.

Ministry of Culture and Recreation (Ontario), *Resources for Community Groups*, Toronto, 1977.

Mahmoud, Syyed T., Gosh, Amit K., eds., **Handbook on Community Economic Development**, Community Research Group, The East Los Angeles Community Union (TELACU), February 1979.

5

Discovering Resources

What are resources? What forms do they take? Where do they come from? How do you get hold of them? When your group begins to search for resources, it will want to identify project bases – i.e. local resources capable of generating revenue. Once these 'primary' resources have been identified, a second search will begin – this time for the resources that will develop your project ideas into ongoing success stories. This chapter will explore the possibilities of community resources, resources from the public sector, and resources from the private sector.

> *"We're great at exploiting resources – that's one of our strong points for sure . . . We know how to make good use of experts and we're good at communicating – at developing an appropriate image of what we are for the people we speak to. A lot of it is bending the system – knowing the system and making it bend, so we can get what we need. . ."*
> – Member. Is Five Foundation.

Money is only one resource. For community economic development groups, the location and development of non-monetary resources are crucial. Resources such as knowledge, skills, experience given voluntarily, or equipment and machinery provided on a trade or loan basis, are essential for running projects. The ability to survive on a very limited budget frequently depends on the creative use of non-monetary resources.

Community economic development projects are not primarily dependent on any one sector of the economy, but instead strive to make equal use of the resources of the formal economy (which includes the private and public sectors), and the informal economy (which is based on community resources). Community economic development's comprehensive approach to resource use places it within the third sector of economic activity. [Chapter 1 discusses this idea more fully.]

Non-monetary resources are called 'technical assistance'. Monetary resources are referred to as 'capital'. Both are essential to successful community economic development. Community-based economic projects try to minimize their need for capital resources, but it is not really possible to carry on business without them. Unfortunately, one of the problems projects face is the perennial difficulty of raising adequate amounts of money.

> *"Capitalization for the third sector? We've found it's pretty much non-existent . . ."*
> – Member, Is Five Foundation.

> *"If there's problems here, it's because of management. We don't have trained people."*
> – Member, Nimpkish Band Council.

When community economic development projects have failed, lack of appropriate technical assistance has been a cause just as often as lack of available capital. In fact, the high failure rate of small businesses in Canada is commonly attributed to poor management, which is another way of stating the same problem.

> *"Almost everyone dreams of owning a business. But too often these dreams turn into financial nightmares. About 70 percent of all new businesses fail within the first five years."*
> – Ministry of Consumer and Commercial Relations, *Starting a Small Business*, 1979.

Very few people who undertake a small business, non-profit community venture or commercial enterprise, have the wide range of skills needed for successful management. Technical assistance, in the form of advice, opportunities for acquiring new knowledge and skills, good written information, and the temporary loan of expertise for on-the-job training purposes, is of crucial importance. Such technical assistance is not readily available.

For community economic development groups, it is particularly difficult to find good technical assistance – i.e. help that takes into account the normal needs of small businesses and the special requirements of non-profit community organizations. Community economic development groups generally need technical assistance in the following areas: management, accounting, organizational development, marketing, needs assessment, evaluation and the development of new businesses.

Community economic development groups need resources – both capital and technical. Every group experiences difficulty in getting adequate and appropriate supplies. On the other side of the coin, however, every established group has been successful in finding and effectively using resources.

> *"These 'make work' projects aren't going to go on forever . . . Canada's in the hole for sixty billion [dollars]. Someday, the bills have got to be paid . . . So at our pasture, we strive to run it on a business-like basis."*
> – Member, Mira Pasture Co-op.

Community Resources

The community is the primary source of goods and services given on a barter or loan basis. These are the resources of the informal economy. A vast input of volunteer time, energy and expertise goes into most community economic development projects. Volunteers often provide reliable professional help in such areas as accounting and law; they also assist with the small, time-consuming and monotonous – but essential – tasks involved in day-to-day operations. In times of crisis, voluntary help often comes from unexpected sources, as happened for the Mira Pasture Co-op, when a fire started after everyone had gone home for the day:

> *"This fellow wasn't even a member. But he was driving by and he saw the smoke. There's no phone out there, so he found a nail, started up the bulldozer, and got the fire under control. Then he went and called the fire brigade. If it hadn't been for him, we'd have lost our barn . . ."*
> – Member, Mira Pasture Co-op.

Your community is your major source of loaned equipment and facilities. Without the loan of meeting space, work space, tools and machinery, many projects would never get off the ground. This was certainly the case for the Codroy Valley. Organizers of the woollen mill were unable to find a suitable site for the planned mill. Finally one of the members of the Rural Development Association decided that he would be willing to sell some of his own land. In his words: "My family owned it. We would never sell our land normally, but since the project was having difficulty finding a place, we thought we should do it."

It is not just in the early stages of your project that community resources are important. Most community economic development groups continue to use community facilities even after they are well-established. In turn, they make their resources available to other community groups. This kind of exchange is not only practical for day-to-day operations; it also helps groups to remain in close contact with their support base – the community.

The Hub is a community business in Almonte, Ontario. Second hand clothing stores like the Hub can generate revenues from a community resource – old clothing – and then use those profits to provide needed services.

> *"We're going to get a proper sign. We want to make it a community thing, not just for the members. Other people – we want their contribution too. Public relations is important."*
> – Member, Mira Pasture Co-op.

1. Your Board of Directors

When community economic development groups elect or appoint a board of directors, it is essential that they be community members. *Projects cannot be effectively directed by 'outside' people.* Groups have found that the priorities of non-local board members are not the same as those of community members. The tension generated by these differing priorities creates problems that are practical as well as philosophical. The best approach is to involve sympathetic outsiders in an advisory or staff capacity, but not as directors.

> *"We started off with a committee [directing the mill] that was one-half us; one-half representatives of the Department of Rural Development. Last year, we decided we were better off on our own . . . If you're doing it yourself, it'll be done a lot better."*
> – Member, Codroy R.D.A.

2. Local Funding Sources

Community resources are not always non-monetary. In fact, every community co-op or credit union is founded on the individual contributions of its members.

> *"Meanwhile nearly everybody had some money in the bank. There was capital in the Community, but the community was unable to use it. The answer was to create their own financial institution in order to pool their individual savings."*
> – CCEC Credit Union brochure.

In almost every community economic development project, members of the core group make financial contributions to the project, either by providing personal guarantees on loans taken out in the name of the project, or by actually donating or loaning money. During the early years of Is Five, for example, there were times of severe shortages. Financial commitments from the core group pulled them through.

> *"There wasn't any money and Jack and I had to take part-time jobs to pay people's salaries . . . We were driving cab at night . . . It really built loyalties."*
> – Member, Is Five Foundation.

It is not uncommon either for community members who are not core group members to make financial contributions. They purchase memberships, attend benefits and participate in fund-raising activities.

3. Service Clubs

Kiwanis, Lions Club, Rotary and Kinsmen are just some of the service clubs that have branches in many Canadian communities. In smaller communities, volunteer firemen, church groups and recreational clubs/associations – e.g. snowmobilers – also act as service clubs. In spite of many differences, c.e.d. groups and service clubs are both working for community betterment. It is important to keep these groups informed about the activities of your organization. Service clubs can be an excellent source of 'loaned' facilities, organizational help for community events, and volunteer labour for community projects. However, since community economic development is likely to be considered a strange idea by most of these groups, be prepared to work at developing a relationship. Offer – several times if necessary – to come to a meeting and explain what you are doing, and why. If you request assistance and are refused, be sure to find out the reason for the refusal, and try to clear up any misunderstanding that may be behind it.

4. The United Way

Some communities have a yearly fund-raising drive for local voluntary organizations, such as the United Way. Community economic development groups are not eligible to join most United Way drives, since they are trying to generate an independent funding base. Some groups decide against participation, even when they are eligible, because they want to avoid having the public image of a charitable organization. Other groups decide to participate because it can help to build a positive public image for their organization, and reassure community members that their group really is working for community benefit in a non-profit way.

5. Labour Organizations

Find out which unions are active in your community. Make a point of talking to local union members and ensuring that they understand what your group is doing. Some community economic development groups have been criticized by unions. Labour organizations sometimes assume that groups operate like sheltered workshops – i.e. that they pay wages below minimum standards. Others are concerned that by receiving public sector funds, community economic development groups may be undercutting the private sector.

In fact, neither of these concerns apply. Community economic development organizations and unions have many similar goals; principally, the provision of local jobs that provide productive work in safe conditions at fair wages. In the United States, one of the largest c.e.d. organizations – a community development corporation called The East Los Angeles Community Union (TELACU) – was started by the United Auto Workers, which is one of North America's bigger unions.

Large unions are often wealthy. They can be approached for financial assistance. Most unions, however – especially small Canadian unions – have no extra funds. They can offer useful services, such as the use of facilities, and training and organizational help, but are unlikely to give any financial assistance.

6. Churches

Churches will provide some funding to community-based activities. These funds are usually dispersed at the regional or national level. The procedure for applying is the same as with foundations and corporations. Work through your local churches whenever you can, using personal contacts and your network of local support. Five churches have united into one organization – PLURA – for the purpose of funding community projects. PLURA has a representative in every province, in addition to a national office.*

7. Fund-raising through Municipalities

Some community economic development groups ask their local municipalities for financial support. Whether this is a good strategy or not depends on your particular group and community. Many groups have policies of avoiding any kind of direct involvement with local political bodies, either through party activity or through association with an elected body. They want to avoid being affected by elections as much as possible. Others feel that monetary support from a township, village or city council is very important, since it indicates approval of the group's activities by a locally-elected body. Such approval can help to generate greater local support and satisfy outside funders that an organization's goals are genuinely community-oriented. Municipalities usually provide token support only. Their major contribution is providing leverage – i.e. the effect that their support can have on other levels of government.

8. The Importance of Community Resources

Locally-available resources and local needs provide the most reliable bases for project selection. The resources of your community are the resources that you are most familiar with. Since you have a better idea of their potential, you will be better able to use them effectively. Local resources will also be a valuable source of assistance once you have decided on your project activities.

Sometimes, groups are eager to apply for government grants or other sources of outside support, in order to avoid the potential 'tangles' of local politics – and because they know that local people will be impressed if they bring resources into the community. Often too, groups feel that there are many more resources available outside the community than inside it. This is true. However, getting those outside resources, and doing so without compromising local goals and priorities is always difficult – and often impossible. Once your project is well-established, outside resources can be used more effectively. However, in the first stages of your c.e.d. effort, the *best rule is not to invest time and energy in looking for outside resources, until you are sure that you cannot find them close to home.*

In general, there is much more potential for creatively using locally-available resources than people expect. If your group has explored all the possibilities and still feels there are insufficient resources at the local level, check to see if all the necessary 'groundwork' has been laid. It may be that a lack of

Circulation of Money

In any cash-based (as opposed to barter-based) community, money is always present. Even the poorest community has a significant amount of money in circulation. In poor communities, however, the money leaves nearly as soon as it enters. Simply stated, one of the differences between wealthy communities and poor ones is that money entering a wealthy community circulates within the community many times before it leaves; whereas, a dollar entering a poor community may change hands only once before it leaves. The more each dollar is used within a community, the more benefits it brings. Community economic development groups – by establishing new small businesses and trying to find ways to satisfy local needs using local resources – are trying to capture the dollars coming into their communities and pass them around more often before they leave. Their goal is not just to bring money into the community, but to make maximum use of the money already there, by ensuring that it really circulates before moving on.

understanding at the community level, or a lack of developed support, is your problem. If this is the case, your best approach is to work on these 'prerequisites' first, before attempting to begin a c.e.d. project. On the other hand, there are communities that in fact have very few local resources. These communities will obviously need outside support, before embarking on community economic development.

9. Obtaining Community Resources

Locally-available resources in almost every community go unrecognized or ignored. People often assume that local resources are insufficient in quantity or poor in quality. This may well be true in the case of large-scale developments with goals of generating maximum profits, but not for the small community projects that have goals of generating only modest revenues. The ability to see local resources in a new way is at the heart of many successful community economic development projects.

Exchange Value: Always think about the 'exchange value' of the resource that you need. When you are negotiating for non-community resources, this is not usually a problem. A wealth of letters, proposals, contracts and application forms, duly signed and copied, are generally sent back and forth before a community group receives resources of any kind. At the community level, arrangements are made differently. Agreements for the use of local resources are often verbal, rather than written – and are made without the weeks or months of discussion about 'conditions of use' that are common in other situations.

Since your most reliable sources of assistance will be local, the time taken to investigate and carefully establish the exchange value of local resources is well worthwhile in the long run. *Good relationships, both within your group and throughout your community, determine your group's ability to obtain local resources.* The ability to create a situation where misunderstandings cannot easily happen, or where people do not need to worry about your group taking advantage of them, is an important factor in determining the strength of your local support.

Ownership: Be prepared to carefully investigate 'rights of ownership and use' that exist over local resources. Many communities in Canada, for example, are surrounded by trees but cannot gain access to them, because cutting rights have been leased out to large lumber companies. Similarly, it may be practically impossible to get permission to use tracts of Crown Land, depending on what plans exist for their use. These situations, where local resources are unused but inaccessible, are not necessarily permanent. Permission for certain non-competitive uses of leased lands can sometimes be secured. In some cases, political pressure can 'release' Crown Lands. However, it is not usually an easy process. It requires large amounts of patience, tenacity and paperwork – and there is no guarantee of success.

Identifying Local Resources: Start with your core group members. What are they willing to offer? The Mira Community Pasture is a good example of a project that is built on the voluntary contributions of the co-op members.Their share capital is just the tip of a very large iceberg of donated and loaned resources.

> *"They donated a lot of equipment, and a tremendous amount of other resources too. They knew how to do the things which needed to get done . . . and our president is a county councillor – a tremendous*

community man. You can trace a lot of important things to him. He's a driving force, a very effective leader . . . They've all worked hard. They're all very skillful people, the members . . ."
– Member, Mira Pasture Co-op.

It is very important, however, not to limit yourself to the ideas and resources of your own group members – essential as they are. Community economic development projects take a long time and a lot of energy; you do not want to wear out your group by depending on its internal resources too heavily. If your group is to be successful, it must learn to exchange resources with other individuals and groups. It must also find ways to accommodate and encourage the input of new ideas and energy from people who were not 'founding members' [See Chapter 7, Section A].

"I'm the living proof that you can come to an organization that's already been started, but it's very hard . . ."
– Member, Is Five Foundation.

Many people from the surrounding area have contributed to the development of the Mira Pasture.

The best way to find out what resources are available within your community is to ask. Do not assume that you know. Examine all the possibilities with as little prejudice as possible. Each group member can ask other people (or organizations that s/he is affiliated with), what they might be interested in contributing to your efforts. It is useful if your core group represents many aspects of your community. Then, for example, it is possible for members of your local group, who are also church members, to be the ones to approach the 'church board' for permission to make use of church facilities.

The principle of smallness is especially important in locating and using community resources. In community economic development, as in so many other things, a little bit can help you to go a very long way. *However, make sure that when taking advantage of small amounts of assistance from a variety of sources, your group does not neglect the necessary task of co-ordination.* Your group will need to find a way to keep track of what it is doing right from the beginning. Keeping minutes, that clearly note agreed responsibilities, schedules and alternative arrangements, is one helpful device.

Whenever you make arrangements to obtain a local resource, record them somewhere – either in a letter or in the minutes of your meetings. One of the great advantages of local resources is that they are usually available without large inputs of time and energy. It is important not to abuse this advantage by neglecting to set down what the conditions of the arrangements are. By noting the arrangements in writing, your group will have a simple record that will allow it to establish the exchange value of what it has received.

Public Sector Resources

Public sector resources come from the various levels of government – local, regional, provincial or federal. Their availability varies greatly, depending on your group's geographical location, its projects and the level of government approached.

1. Programmes for Community Economic Development

Although federal, provincial and some local governments see themselves as having a role to play in local economic development, there are at present no programmes organized specifically to assist the kind of small-scale, community-based initiatives that this book describes. Change is in the wind. City governments in Toronto and Halifax are making efforts to assist community-based economic efforts. Several provinces, including Newfoundland, Quebec and Saskatchewan, have adopted programmes that have goals of assisting locally-controlled social and economic development efforts. The revived federal LEDA programme*, although oriented specifically to job creation, may also prove to be useful in this respect. However, programmes that provide support for projects in social development, economic development, cultural enhancement, community education and the development of small businesses do exist. These are the progrogrammes that c.e.d. organizations are currently using.

2. The Role of the Public Sector

The kind of role that governments play changes with the political climate. Keeping this in mind, we have tried to provide a general guide, by identifying the roles that governments have played in the past in the following areas:

a) research costs;
b) start-up costs;
c) purchase of fixed assets;
d) operating costs; and,
e) expansion and improvement costs.

Research Costs

Government loans or grants that provide money to pay the cost of identifying and developing a project idea, are usually described as 'funds for needs assessment', planning or feasibility studies, design development, or small business development. At the federal level, groups/programmes such as the National Research Council, the Department of Industry, Trade and Commerce, and the LEAP programme have provided such assistance in the past. At the provincial level, funds have been made available through such groups as Newforndland's Department of Rural Development or Saskatchewan's Department of Northern Development – or through ministries that have an interest in the content of a particular project. Some groups have also made use of short-term job creation initiatives, such as the summer and student employment programmes. The short duration and low salaries of these programmes mean that as a rule, they can only be used in situations not requiring complex or highly technical research.

Groups such as Is Five and Contact have been able to make use of research and development, and demonstration grants from the ministries of Industry, Trade and Commerce, National Health and Welfare, and Regional Economic Expansion. The problem with these grants is that – by definition – they can only be given once for a particular purpose. Your project must therefore be sufficiently unique – i.e. considered distinct from anything else that has been or is being done. As a result, although they are well-suited to the research needs of c.e.d. organizations, development or demonstration grants are not often available.

Some groups, rather than applying for money, arrange to get professional help. Colleges and universities can be useful in this respect. The Bras D'Or Institute of the College of Cape Breton, for example, sponsored a needs assessment survey that aided the development of the Mira Community Pasture. Counsellors, who are skilled in research, are sometimes available at a low cost from the CASE programme of the Federal Business Development bank (F.B.D.B.). Canadian Executive Service Overseas (C.E.S.O.) provides assistance to native groups on a similar basis.

Start-up Costs

Almost every group requires external inputs of money and/or resources –i.e. venture capital – to cover the costs of its first months/years of operation. Assistance is needed to cover: rent; purchase of inventory; and equipment and operating costs – including salaries, publicity and advertising. Securing adequate amounts of venture capital has not generally been easy for c.e.d. groups. Most groups do not qualify for small business loans (available through the F.B.D.B. or provincial development corporations/departments), because of their non-profit status, small size and generally unorthodox approach to creating small enterprises. For the most part, public sector sources of venture capital have been limited to job creation programmes, or research and demonstration grants. When good technical assistance is available, most groups can find ways to minimize start-up costs. For example, some make use of fiscal policies that provide tax incentives, training allowances or wage subsidies for the creation of new jobs.

Purchase of Fixed Assets

Money to buy equipment and machinery is also hard to come by. The public sector is occasionally willing to provide funds for these purposes as a 'lender of last resort', or as part of a larger project, but in general this is the private sector's 'territory'. LEAP, for example, provides limited capital funding based on the number of jobs created. Demonstration grants also take into account the acquisition of equipment and facilities. When large and expensive pieces of equipment are needed for a limited time period only, arrangements can occasionally be made to borrow them from public sources. This kind of loan is almost always dependent upon the existence of a sympathetic public sector employee, who is willing to 'deviate' from normal routines.

Operating Costs:

The biggest item under operating costs is usually wages – although operating costs do include all the day-to-day administrative and co-ordinating costs of your organization. Federal and provincial job creation funds can sometimes be used to offset salary costs. These grants and subsidies are usually only available when new employees are being hired, or occasionally when existing employees are being trained for new positions. This is only a short-term proposition that pays salaries which are usually close to the minimum wage level. Some social development programmes, such as LEAP or Health and Welfare demonstration grants, do provide core funding to cover operating costs for periods of up to three years (they have even given support on occasion for up to four or five years).

The solution to the problem of core funding lies as much in the areas of organization and management as it does in the availability of resources. As with start-up costs, experienced and competent management can make a significant difference. It is sometimes possible to second people from government departments or educational institutions for six months to a year. When it works well, this can be an excellent arrangement, but it is necessary to find someone who is both willing and competent enough to work on a community-oriented project. Such people are not always easy to find. Many do not have the necessary patience and skills to be able to work in a 'non-professional' setting.

Groups can sometimes minimize operating costs by taking advantage of government fiscal policies, such as tax allowances to non-profit or educational groups, or municipal 'tax breaks'.

> *"It would help us to be in a community where local government supported manufacturing . . . There would be tax breaks . . . Kingston is more of a government and service town."*
> – Employee, Comfort Clothing Services.

Although most c.e.d. groups have little choice with respect to location, it is well worthwhile looking into municipal incentives for newly-located businesses. Sometimes too, it is possible to arrange to make use of public facilities such as unused office space at little or no cost. A sympathetic municipality can be of great assistance, not only by arranging access to their own facilities, but also by helping to arrange use of regional, provincial or federal facilities.

Expansion and Improvement Costs: When a c.e.d. project decides to expand or improve an enterprise, or to take on a new venture, it usually requires additional resources. Purchasing new equipment, breaking into a new market, or adding new activities all have costs in terms of time, money and skill development. Once a community economic development group has a good track record – i.e. a history reflecting some success, including an ongoing enterprise or two – securing resources generally becomes less difficult.

Loans and development grants for the design, implementation and monitoring of new projects are available through programmes sponsored by the National Research Council (N.T.E.P.), and Industry, Trade and Commerce (D.R.E.C.T.).* The federal government and several of the provinces have programmes that provide assistance to established small businesses, although – once again – being small and non-profit can pose a problem. Energy-related businesses, because of the current importance of energy issues, can also find various types of assistance at the federal and provincial levels.

Groups involved in non-profit businesses have a great need for competent technical assistance when they reach the expansion/improvement stage. Good advice about how to use available funds and how to develop organizations becomes crucial. As organizations grow and change, sophisticated levels of technical knowledge and new approaches to management become necessary. Unfortunately, there is very little good technical assistance available for community economic development groups. Programmes such as CASE are few and far between, and are often inadequate for meeting the special needs of groups with social and economic goals. Most groups turn to the private sector, but there too, relatively little is available.

3. Obtaining Public Resources

Public resources are political resources. Your ability to obtain these resources may be just as dependent on external factors such as which parties your provincial and federal representatives belong to – as it is on the 'qualifications' of your c.e.d. project. When you apply for money or technical assistance from a particular public programme, it is important to know why that programme was created initially – e.g. whether it was designed to represent a particular interest (such as agriculture), or to lessen a potentially damaging condition (such as unemployment or regional underdevelopment). Try to 'fit' your application to a framework that people working in a particular programme or ministry are used to – it is much more likely to be supported if you do.

Developing Networks: Within every government – provincial, federal and municipal – there are sympathetic and knowledgeable civil servants or municipal employees. The problem is to find them. Word of mouth and personal contacts are the only reliable methods for doing so. When you are considering going to a particular government body for assistance, take the time to ask members of other groups who they have dealt with, and who might be interested in what you are trying to do. Even if the person suggested does not have a job that relates directly to your 'need', his or her position on the 'inside' of the agency may well mean you will receive some useful tips. Since knowing your group's interests and needs enables them to do a better job of making the programmes they work on more responsive to communities, these people will usually be happy to hear from you.

Writing Your Proposal:

In order to apply for public resources or to foundations, you will need a clear, well-written proposal. Before you start, decide how detailed your proposal should be. Generally speaking, the more assistance you are asking for, the longer your proposal will be. Find out as much as you can about the department or foundation you are applying to before you draw up your proposal. Try to find another community group or individual who has worked with your 'prospect' before. Such people can tell you something about how and when decisions are made, what the track record on decisions is, how information is communicated, and what kinds of problems you are likely to run into.

Talk to someone who works in the government department where you intend to apply. Programmes – and their criteria – change constantly. Save yourself the time and effort involved in submitting proposals and applications, by making sure you know beforehand that your project has some chance of receiving support. Proposals to government agencies will usually be longer than proposals to foundations. However, whatever the length, it will include the following sections.

The people of Alert Bay originally wrote the NIDA plan as a proposal for Habitat funding.

a) Background

Start by *introducing* your organization. Talk about how and when it got started, your goals and significant activities up until now. If your organization is new, describe some of the past accomplishments of people who are members. Concentrate on activities related to your goals. Indicate who supports you, including other organizations and prominent people. If you think it is appropriate, attach letters of support or related newspaper articles to your proposals as appendices. It is always a good idea to keep a file of 'supporting evidence' like this on hand. Give some idea of why your organization is particularly well-suited to undertaking the proposed project. Be honest and brief, but not too modest. Think about what will impress your potential funder. Include information that will establish or enhance your credibility with the group you are approaching.

Next, identify the *rationale* for your proposal. Briefly describe your community and its location. You may want to include a map. State the need or problem your project will address. Be as specific as possible. Avoid the temptation to over-emphasize the problem. You do not want to make your situation sound hopeless. Your proposal should sound sincerely concerned, but positive about the possibility for improvement. Give some evidence that illustrates the problem. Statistics, statements from respected individuals or organizations, and photographs or other visual materials are often useful. Describe how your organization became involved in the idea for the project. Show the connection between your goals and the stated problem. What brought your group to the point of writing a proposal for funds?

b) Goals

Describe what your project is designed to do about the stated problem. Be as specific as possible. Your goals should provide an impact – i.e. they should identify the difference your project will make, for example, to reducing unemployment among youth, or to increasing the productivity of part-time farmers. Your goals should be clear and, whenever possible, measurable. They are the yardsticks you will use to evaluate your project.

c) Strategies

Describe your project activities. Make sure that they clearly relate to your goals. State why you have chosen these particular activities, as opposed to alternative methods. 'Objective' evidence – statements from other groups or organizations, statistics or results from previous programmes will be useful. Often you will want to describe how your methods will make the best use of available resources. Show that your ideas are the result of careful planning and research. Include a detailed schedule or plan.

d) Evaluation measures

State how you will know if you have achieved your goals. Try to identify 'objective' measures – evidence that is not based just on personal opinions. If the project is small – e.g. producing and distributing a book – it can probably be evaluated by your organization itself. Your evidence can be based on the actual product (in this case a book), and on its degree of usefulness (e.g. how well the book sells to the identified market). If your project is large – and especially if it is costly – you may want to hire an outside evaluator. Colleges, universities and some social service organizations may be able to offer you this service.

e) Follow-up

If the project is to be carried on, describe your plans for the future. In particular, state how you expect to fund the project on an ongoing basis. Where appropriate, you will want to include statements of expected income from the project over a three to five year period, showing how your project will become self-sufficient.

f) Budget

Here's one way to organize your budget

Time period covered:

Projected Expenses

Start-up Costs:
- preliminary research costs

Operating Costs:
- wages and salaries
- benefits
- consultants' fees, contracted services (e.g. bookkeeping)
- staff education/development (e.g. travel and meetings)
- rental of work space
- rent/lease/purchase of equipment (e.g. typewriters)
- supplies (paper, etc.)
- telephone
- heat and hydro
- insurance, licences, etc.
- postage
- advertising and promotion
- other (add 5 to 10 percent for unanticipated costs)

Total Expenses:

Projected Revenues

Project Income (sales, fees, etc.)
Grants
Subsidies
Donations
Donated Equipment or Services (identify donors by name)

Total Revenues:

Place a dollar value on any donated or loaned equipment, labour or other services you expect to receive. The value of these donations will show up in your expense column in the appropriate category; and in your revenue column, under donated equipment and services. The more you can acquire through informal (non-monetary) means, the better. Usually, the difference between your costs and your expected revenues will be the amount of money you are asking for.

g) Summary and covering letter

Your summary should be short and very clear. Tell who you are, the purpose of your project, what its results will be, and what your funding requirements are. The summary should be the first thing that your potential funder sees. You may want to incorporate it into your covering letter. Write a personal covering letter. Do not send a form letter. In addition to summarizing your proposal, you should indicate in your letter why you are approaching this particular funder.

Sound as convincing as possible. Be realistic, but also be positive and confident. Review your draft proposal. Avoid using tentative words like 'seem', 'attempt', 'try' or 'maybe'. Show your draft to someone who is not a member of your organization, and ask for their ideas. Most government departments will provide you with an outline or application form telling you what they expect. Books on writing proposals are available in most libraries.* However, the best advice comes from people who have written proposals before – e.g. members of other community organizations, or local municipal employees such as your township clerk.

After your proposal has been submitted, follow it up with a phone call and a personal meeting. If your group is not able to meet personally with the people who will be reviewing your proposal, it is sometimes possible to have someone else – such as your local Member of Parliament – do so on your behalf. However, this should not be considered a standard or desirable practice. Use your network. A phone call on your behalf by a sympathetic civil servant can be very useful in finding out what chance your proposal has.

4. Managing Public Resources

"People in government – they're not easy to work with . . . they lose invoices, take months to answer questions, phone you up to say this is wrong and that is wrong . . . Picky, picky, picky."
– Member, Is Five Foundation.

Controls and Accountability:

If your proposal is accepted, you will still have lots of work ahead of you. The need for detailed accounts of where the money is being spent means that government resources inevitably entail a lot of writing, bookkeeping, meetings and phone calls. Many government programmes make a real attempt to minimize the work they ask groups to do. Others do not. Even those that make this effort still demand an awesome amount of paperwork and discussion. Government departments also expect to be able to use your project as as showpiece, if it goes well. If you make it clear that you want as few visitors or as little publicity as possible, most government representatives will heed your wishes – but they do need to be warned in advance.

Programmes – or their criteria – can change at any time. New requests – i.e. asking you to change or add activities after a project proposal has been approved – are not unusual. Groups are sometimes afraid to say no, in case they might jeopardize present or future funding. When it is your turn, squelch this fear. If the request does not fit into your plans, be prepared to be firm. *Many groups have suffered needlessly because of costly mistakes made in trying to satisfy funders who were unfamiliar with local conditions.* Remember that these public resources have been applied for and granted as sources of assistance, not hindrance. Most government representatives are quite willing to have you argue with them on this basis.

Funds, once granted, are seldom withdrawn quickly, except in cases of embezzlement. However, the possibility of future funding involves so many circumstances beyond your control, that it is never wise to sacrifice your project goals. The most important thing is to maintain control over your project. Always be able to say: "It's ours".

Private Sector Resources

The private sector controls many resources that are important to the economy at every level. The success of community economic development groups rests just as much on their ability to develop good working relationships with the private sector, as it does on their ability to work with the public sector and their own communities. Such is the nature of third sector organizations.

Private sector organizations that are important to community economic development include financial institutions, banks and credit unions, charitable organizations attached to corporations, and foundations. Private sector support for c.e.d. varies considerably. The attitude of individual businessmen towards community betterment, and the size of a business, are important factors. Communities that are small, or have many small businesses in them, receive more 'direct' assistance than large communities, or communities dominated by large enterprises (e.g. single resource towns). Although in a few cases large companies have involved themselves in the planning and development of all aspects of community life, for the most part, corporations have remained aloof from the communities that surround their mines and mills. However, regardless of size, communities in which large corporations are active are more likely to receive donations from foundations or corporate charities, than are communities in which the corporations have little or no direct interest.

1. Small Business

In some ways, the experiences c.e.d. groups have had with soliciting private sector resources are similar, no matter what their community is like. Most groups have managed to find a few local businessmen who are interested in community economic development. Their participation as board members, advisors and providers of various services, ranging from accounting to construction contracting, has been invaluable.

2. Big Business

The involvement of large-scale corporations in supporting community initiatives is minimal in relation to the vast resources they control. For example, in 1976, United States corporate grants amounted to roughly 1% of pre-tax profits. This figure included donations to hospitals, The United Way, etc. [Mitiguy, 1978]. Recently, some corporations have started to become more sensitive to the social and environmental costs of production. Although this growing sense of social responsibility has yet to be felt in the form of increasing support for community organizations, it may be that large corporations will eventually become more interested in community efforts. Such involvement could turn out to be something of a mixed blessing. After all, the primary goal of the private sector is to generate profits through increasing control over production capacities and markets. It is very important for c.e.d. groups to remember that the private sector, like the public sector, will act in its own interests. Sometimes those interests will overlap with those of community economic development organizations, but often they will not.

3. Financial Institutions

Unlike other resource groups, financial institutions – like your local bank – will have only a secondary interest in the social value of your project. Their assessment will be based on the profit-making potential of your efforts. There are exceptions – e.g. credit unions like CCEC – where social goals and social impacts will be just as important as profits.

CCEC Lending Policy

The main topic of discussion at the CCEC Credit Union's first general meeting on April 28, 1976, was loan policy. The members decided that both group and individual loans were important. It was resolved that loans should meet people's *needs* and not necessarily their *wants*.

Some of the activities that our present lending policy encourages are: education, ecological concerns, social action, health care, food, shelter, child care and collectively owned enterprises.

At present the interest rate on most loans is 10 percent. There is a special 8 percent rate for loans which help people working co-operatively to provide services to credit union members or the community as a whole. Included in this special 8 percent rate are loans for the purchase of shares in a co-operative. The interest rates reflect the actual cost of operating the credit union, and plans call for the rates to decrease as the credit union grows larger.

If you would like additional information on the lending policy, please contact the Loans Officer or a member of the Credit Committee.

– CCEC Credit Union brochure.

There are other kinds of financial institutions in addition to banks and credit unions – e.g. finance companies and venture capital companies. If for no other reason, community enterprises' low rate of profit generation, and the high rate of return demanded by finance companies, make them incompatible partners. Venture capital companies limit themselves to large developments – usually involving initial investments of more than $100,000. We have yet to talk to any people involved in c.e.d. projects in Canada who have made use of financial organizations other than banks and credit unions.

4. Foundations and Corporate Charities

Foundations and corporations will be interested in how your project fits in with their image and their requirements. Financial potential may be a consideration, but your project's goals of community betterment will be looked at first. Securing funds from large foundations or corporations is usually time-consuming and complicated, but funds once granted come with no strings attached – other than an acknowledgement of the source and an assurance that the money will be used for the purpose for which it was granted.

Grants from large foundations can be substantial – e.g. in the $10,000 to $100,000 range. Most foundations, however, are small family establishments, giving a few annual grants in the $500 to $5,000 range. Grants often come on a matching basis. For example, if your appeal is for $10,000, a foundation may grant you $5,000, pending assurance that you have raised the remaining amount. Groups can sometimes use the dollar value of donated services to make up part of their 'matching' requirements.

5. Consultants

Professional consultants are another private sector resource. These people make their living by offering advice on business management, programme development, enterprise feasibility, programme evaluation, and a host of other social and economic problems. Their services are usually expensive. Before your group hires a consultant, make sure that you cannot get the information you need from local sources.

6. The Role of the Private Sector

As we did when discussing the public sector's role, we will summarize the kinds of roles that the private sector has played in community economic development efforts:

Research Costs:

Financial assistance for research is sometimes available from foundations or through corporate donations. Technical assistance with research is available from banks and credit unions when they are considering a loan request from your group. Some voluntary support for research comes from people working in business organizations. Business organizations are often good sources of information about ratios and standards applicable to various businesses. Consultants will sometimes provide some research help on a barter basis, but you should expect to pay for anything other than general information.

Start-up Costs:

As with research funds, financial involvement by the private sector for 'start-up' is usually limited to donations from foundations and corporations. Venture capital corporations, that invest in new businesses, generally limit themselves to investments over $100,000, and often take an equity position in those businesses. For these reasons, and because venture capital corporations are few in number, c.e.d. groups in Canada have not so far been involved with them.

The model, however, of the venture capital corporation or holding company, is one that has appealed to many community development corporations. Groups such as Nanaimo's Community Employment Advisory Society* are trying to develop small-scale, locally-based venture capital corporations as tools for community economic development.

Technical assistance during start-up comes mainly in the form of advice from members of the business community, business organizations, banks and credit unions. These people often represent your best sources of assistance at this stage.

Purchase of Fixed Assets:

Loans to purchase equipment and machinery are available from banks and credit unions. However, banks and many credit unions are reluctant to invest in high-risk ventures – i.e. businesses that are less than five years old, and/or projects that are considered unusual (e.g. constructing solar collectors). Small credit unions are often willing to be more flexible in extending loans to their members. However, their small size means that loans are only available in relatively small amounts.

Operating Costs:

A line of credit is an arrangement with a bank or credit union that allows for regular overdrafts. Most businesses finance their operating costs in part by obtaining a floating line of credit. The amount of credit offered is determined by the bank or credit union. It is usually a percentage of the group's liquid assets – inventories and accounts receivable (i.e. payments owed to them), that are relatively easy to convert to money if necessary. As with other kinds of loans, banks and credit unions may be reluctant to allow a line of credit to new businesses, or to businesses that are non-profit – or otherwise 'atypical'.

Foundations and corporations usually do not provide grants to cover the operating costs of a project as such. However, they will include an allowance for operating costs in the budget of projects they grant support to.

Expansion and Improvement Costs: A business that has been in existence for a minimum of three years, has a track record of paying its bills and generating increasing revenues, and can present a sound business plan, is eligible for a loan from a bank or credit union. Whether the business will actually receive a loan or not depends on many factors, such as: the exact nature of the information on its balance sheets, and statements of profit and loss; its age and status in the community; its historical relationship with the financial institution it is approaching; and the lending policies of that particular bank or credit union.

Foundations and corporations will occasionally give grants for expansion or improvement. In general, though, they prefer to fund new or innovative projects, rather than to provide support to something that is already ongoing. The best technical assistance usually comes from members of the business community, either on a voluntary or 'fee-for-service' basis. For example, your accountant, if s/he has a history of involvement in your organization, can often be of assistance when your group is considering expanding its projects.

7. Obtaining Private Sector Resources

How you negotiate for private sector resources varies greatly, depending on which part of the private sector you are approaching. We'll look at them one at a time:

Foundations: Most libraries have reference books that list foundations and grant-giving agencies. These books give addresses to write to, list criteria or interest areas for each foundation, and often give indications of the size of grants that a foundation normally gives. The foundations are not all covered, but books like **The Canadian Directory to Foundations and Granting Agencies*** provide a good starting point.

The best way to approach foundations is to send a personal letter – two pages or less in length – that briefly describes the background, purpose, goals, activities and resource needs of your project. Then telephone the foundation, if possible. Try to arrange a personal interview, but only if you feel that there is a good chance the foundation will be interested in your project. Remember that foundations receive hundreds of proposals each year and grant funds to very few of them.

If a foundation is interested in your proposal, it will ask for additional information – e.g. a detailed description of proposed activities, a complete budget and names of other funding organizations you have applied to. If a foundation expresses initial interest in your project, but ultimately does not fund it, ask its representative to refer you to other groups who might be willing to do so.

A Checklist . . .

As you prepare your submission, and before you send it off to a potential donor, check with this list and make sure that you have done everything and included everything necessary.

Looking for Money:

1. Research possible donors.
2. Have you arranged for a charitable donations number or a trustee of funds?
3. Your submission. Have you included:
   - a personal letter to the donor
   - the name, address and telephone number of your organization
   - the purpose of your organization
   - your charitable donations number or trustee arrangements
   - the name of the person in charge of the proposed project
   - the background of your proposal
   - its goals
   - how you plan to reach those goals
   - the names of groups working with you
   - how long your project will take
   - the amount of money being requested
   - your contribution to the project
   - the reason your organization is involved
   - an annual report, including financial reports
   - a detailed budget of the project
   - a one-page summary, if necessary
4. Is your information clear? Would it make sense to someone who does not know anything about the area under discussion?
5. Is your information honest?
6. Is the submission neat and free from spelling and grammatical errors?
7. Is it polite? Does it request a grant or demand one?

Two Months Later

If you have not received a reply, write again.

When Additional Information is Requested

Provide it promptly.

When You Are Turned Down

Write and thank the organization for considering your request.

When the Money Arrives

Send a personal thank-you letter, enclosing the charitable donations receipt.

Halfway Through the Project

Provide a follow-up report to the donors.

At the End of the Project

Provide a final report on the project, including a financial report. If applicable, comment on the specific use of that donor's grant.

– Extract from *A Fund-raising Guide for Native Groups*, by Lynda Cronin, 1977, p.21.

Corporations: Try to find corporations that have a history of donations, and a purpose in some way related to yours. In Toronto, for example, several of the large commercial radio stations support CJRT – a non-profit station – because it provides programming that the commercial stations approve of but do not air (for financial reasons). Corporations differ widely in the way they handle donations. Some have set up foundations (like Ford or Kellogg), or charities that dispense large amounts of money. Others hire someone – who usually handles several different companies – to screen applications and make recommendations. The most common arrangement is to delegate an employee of the company – e.g. the president, public relations officer or executive secretary – to handle requests for donations.

Use personal contacts if at all possible when you approach a corporation. Be prepared to back up your request with a written proposal, although sometimes a letter is all that is required. With both foundations and corporations, try to find other groups who have previously received funding from the source you are approaching and ask their advice. *In general, activities relating to areas of mutual concern are the ones most likely to receive support.*

Banks and Credit Unions: Support from banks and credit unions is primarily dependent on financial concerns. It is important to know your local bank or credit union manager, and to have a history of placing your funds (no matter how meagre), in the bank/credit union you approach. Banks and credit unions are in the business of reinvesting money in the interests of their own investors. As a result, they seek to find the best combination of high-profit (i.e. high return on their investment in your project), and low-risk (i.e. low probability that they will lose their money). They will evaluate your proposal in this light.

Before you begin to prepare a loan application, meet with the loans officer at your credit union/bank. Before you go in, try to find out as much as you can about the kinds of services the institution offers. Have an idea of what your financial needs are: short-term or long-term; large or small; and how you intend to use your loan. It is not necessary to be an expert. Your manager sees it as his or her work to provide you with information about the services available to you. Find out if the kind of service you need is available, and on what terms. Find out exactly what kind of information your loan application should include. Institutions differ on certain questions, such as whether unaudited financial statements are acceptable, and whether cash flow projections should be on a monthly or quarterly basis. You may also want to check out other banks and credit unions (if you are eligible for membership). There is stiff competition between financial organizations, and it may be that the bank or credit union across the street can give you better terms than your own.

In order to make a loan application, you will need to prepare a business plan. Like project proposals, business plans vary greatly in length, depending on their use and the amount of financing you want. All business plans include cash flow projections, working capital estimates and financial statements – or, if your enterprise is just starting, pro forma income statements.† Be careful not to underestimate your financial requirements. Asking for too little money is just as much a sign of managerial incompetence in the eyes of

† Pro forma financial statements (e.g. income, balance) are plans which illustrate how you foresee the use of money within your project.

your loans officer, as asking for too much. Almost every new or expanding small business runs into cash flow problems, even with careful financial planning. 'Under financing' is one of the major reasons for the high rate of small business failures. [Dingwall, 1980]

Be Prepared to Discuss:

a) where your business idea came from;
b) what background you and other members of your organization have that makes your group a good and responsible loan risk;
c) your plan for securing all the financial and technical assistance necessary to make your venture a success;
d) your marketing plan;
e) your approach to management, including how responsibility is allocated (take along job descriptions if you have them), and evaluation measures; and,
f) your performance goals for an identified period (usually two years or more), not only in terms of expected revenues, but also in terms of the development of your organization as a whole.

Your accountant and your loans officer can assist you with the preparation of a business plan or loan application, but the onus is on your organization to effectively present your case. When you do go in with your loan application, be confident and assertive. Make sure that you are able to discuss the finances and operations of your community economic development project(s) competently.

8. Developing Your Own Financial Institution

The difficulties that community-based organizations have in raising capital have led to efforts to create new financial institutions, designed specifically to serve particular communities. This is what credit unions are all about. Historically, credit unions are based on a bond of association – a community of members. Credit unions have been organized to serve communities of every type: geographical or interest-based. In addition to credit unions such as the CCEC, there are women's credit unions, trade union credit unions, and in Vancouver, a native people's credit union.

If there are a sufficient number of interested parties to do the work and provide a financial base, a newly organized credit union can provide increased access to financial assistance for members, through the reinvestment of its own funds, and by providing access to central credit union funds and services. Such a project, however, demands vast amounts of time and energy. New credit unions also face the 'dilemma' of being small – i.e. their size limits the kinds of services and loans they can provide. Like other community economic development organizations, they also face the problem of finding a balance between maintaining their philosophical goals and running a viable organization that provides adequate services.

Another type of financial institution that c.e.d. groups are attempting to organize is the venture capital company – or holding company. In the

United States, many community development corporations are organized in this way. In Nanaimo, British Columbia, the Nanaimo Community Employment Advisory Society (N.C.E.A.S.) has plans to provide start-up financing to new local enterprises on favourable terms. Contact, in Quebec, has included a similar mechanism in its plans for the future. For these groups, the problem is having the necessary pool of money to draw from. The N.C.E.A.S. plans to use a government grant as its seed capital. Contact hopes to slowly build a pool of money that can be reinvested in new enterprises through accumulating revenues from contracts for technical assistance.

9. Professional Consultants

A good consultant can be very helpful, either in providing expertise that is not locally available, or in adding legitimacy and credibility to a group's proposal for funding. If a community economic development group is applying to public or private sources for funds in excess of $100,000, a report by a respected outsider is often essential. Many groups, however, have hired consultants and been very disappointed with the results.

If your group is considering hiring a professional consultant, getting your money's worth will involve the following:

1. Be specific about your needs. Before you approach a consultant, make sure that your group is in agreement about what information is needed, and how it will be used. The more specific your questions are, the more likely it is that you will get good information.

2. Think carefully about what kind of consultant you want. Consultants who offer their services to c.e.d. groups will have expertise in business, education or social development – rarely all three. A consultant just starting out will be less expensive, and may take a more active interest in your particular project, but his or her recommendations will probably not impress outside funders in the way that someone from a well-established firm, with lots of 'successes' behind him/her, will.

3. Consider several consultants before hiring. Try to interview at least two before going ahead. Make sure that the people in your group will like the person you are considering well enough to be willing to talk freely to him/her. Ask for documentation – i.e. samples of reports prepared previously. Contact at least two groups who have previously used the consultant and ask for their opinions. Do not be shy about asking for this information if it is not offered. Consultants know that their survival depends on having clients who are satisfied with their services. A good consultant will be just as concerned as you are that the services s/he can offer will be appropriate to your particular needs.

4. When you have selected one or two likely prospects, and have clearly indicated to the consultant what you want, ask for a letter summarizing what the consultant will offer. The letter should state:
   - i) What form the final product will take.
   - ii) How the work will be carried out – including how much time the consultant will spend with you, who will be consulted, and what other sources of information will be used.
   - iii) What the work schedule will be.
   - iv) What the cost will be, and whether it will cover such things as xerox-

ing, phone calls, office space, secretarial services and transportation.

v) What kind of follow-up there will be, and what it will cost – i.e. if the consultant recommends a specific strategy, or identifies a particular need – e.g. a restructured accounting system – can s/he assist with this task?

5. Your response to this letter should be in writing. Identify changes or possible sources of confusion clearly, and ask for a second letter that incorporates them. This letter can usually serve as a contract – if you wish.

6. Be wary of any consultant who does not want to go through this process. Be sure to find out why.

7. Inexpensive consulting services are sometimes available through universities or colleges. Since these services often involve students or academics who also teach, it is especially important to be very specific about your needs. Accuracy of scheduling and quality of work may vary unpredictably. Check these services out carefully. They can be a good source of assistance.

10. Appropriate Resources

"LEAP doesn't really seem to know what the right steps are to let us be an independent business . . . Like most small businesses we have cash flow problems – because LEAP will leave us with no operating capital when their funding stops, we could be in a serious bind."
– Employee, Comfort Clothing Services.

"LEAP is a job creation programme – a social development programme, not a programme to start small businesses."
– Former LEAP Project Officer.

Community economic development groups have real problems in finding resources that are appropriate to their needs. Where profit is a means, rather than an end, the private sector is reluctant to become involved. Where 'business' is a strategy for the achievement of social or cultural goals, the public sector feels it has no place. Within both sectors, there is skepticism about the ability of people to control and manage their own affairs.

"I'm generally skeptical of governments using groups like ours to achieve their own goals . . . The groups get their agenda changed by the money-givers."
– Member, Mira Pasture Co-op.

Resources are never 'free', wherever they come from. Community-based resources are usually accompanied by costs in the form of obligations and responsibilities. Private sector resources expect a monetary return. The price tag on public resources comes in the form of time and energy spent in working for the relevant government department – i.e. making your project part of their programmes. Each resource sector has its inherent problems. Each supplier of resources will, often without realizing it, try to affect the goals of your c.e.d. project. Sometimes their influence is positive. The private sector, for example, with its 'profit first' orientation, can be helpful in pointing out what is really necessary to make money. However, if 'profit first' becomes your orientation, you no longer have a c.e.d. project. For all c.e.d. groups, the challenge is to make the compromises necessary to be able to work with private, public and community resources without losing sight of their own unique goals and methods.

For Further Reading:

Canadian Business magazine publishes in each issue a section with advice for small businesses. See especially Dingwall, James, *Bargaining With Your Banker*, Vol. 53, No. 6, June 1980.

Cronin, Lynda, **A Guide to Fund-raising for Native Groups**, Ottawa, Canadian Association in Support of Native Peoples, 1977.

Mortensen, Dave, chairman, *Work Plan 1980/81: a new community plan in job development*, Nanaimo Community Employment Advisory Society, Nanaimo, B.C., February 1980.

Ministry of Consumer and Commercial Relations (Ontario), *Starting a Small Business*, Toronto, 1979.

Mitiguy, Nancy, **The Rich Get Richer and the Poor Write Proposals**, Boston, Citizen Involvement Publications, 1978.

6

Developing Not-for-Profit Enterprises

Business development is a strategic part of any community-based economic development project. This chapter provides you with a strategy for financial planning and business development. We have divided the discussion into two main sections – project assessment and financial management. Project assessment includes: collecting and analyzing community information; collecting trade information and doing market analysis; collecting and using financial information; and writing a business plan. Financial management includes information on choosing investment options, bookkeeping and preparing annual reports.

The big difference between planning for community economic development and planning for most other community efforts is in the area of financial planning. The trick is to avoid bankruptcy. Community economic development projects must include activities that are profit-making. They must also try to limit their operating costs and non-paying activities, in order not to put too much strain on their finances.

Assess each of your selected activities in terms of its ability to generate revenue. In the beginning, you should engage in activities that will make a profit, or at least breakeven. Once your organization has some experience, it will be in a better position to decide when and how it can take on activities that need to be subsidized.

If your group does not include people with business knowledge, you are at a distinct disadvantage. Good information and advice is often difficult to get. You can start by going to other small business operators who may be sympathetic. Many colleges and universities have small business advisory services. In addition, the Federal Business Development Bank has pamphlets and programmes that may be of help to you.*

The advice that you get may well be laced with contradictions. There are exceptions to every rule, particularly when dealing with small businesses. In the end, your group will have to sort through all the advice you have been given. Try to learn as much as you can from it, then take a deep breath and plunge in. For many groups, the decision to go ahead is based as much on collective intuition and a desire to do what supposedly cannot be done, as on anything else.

> *"I was born on the thirteenth, and I've been swimming upstream ever since. Whenever somebody tells me I can't do something, I'm more than ever determined to do it."*
> – Member, Mira Pasture Co-op.

The 'plunge in and go ahead' route is usually the necessary one for community economic development groups. This approach does not guarantee success, but it does make success possible by moving a group from planning to action.

Project Assessment

> The idea of making clothes especially designed for physically handicapped people had been around for a long time before the start of Comfort Clothing. Large clothing manufacturers were reluctant to create an adaptive clothing sideline, because they knew that it would require a unique approach to marketing. It was not worthwhile for them to reorganize for a comparatively small market – i.e. one that would be unable ever to generate significant revenues. For Comfort Clothing, the presence of this small market – with its 'insignificant' potential revenues – was enough to justify opening a small factory that currently provides thirteen people with employment.

You will require three basic sets of information in order to assess the feasibility of any particular enterprise:
a) socio-economic information about your own community;
b) trade information about the particular business you are considering; and
c) financial information describing where you will raise money and how it will be spent.

Such information is generally already available; original research is rarely necessary. The summary of your information – i.e. *the business plan* – will be useful to you, not only in attracting financing for your project, but also as an important tool in organizing and running your project. Your first enterprises will usually be small and simple, established because there is an obvious need in your community that your organization can fill.

The principle of need provides the basis of every plan for community enterprise development, and will continue to be central to your work in business development no matter how large and complex your projects become.

Even the most straightforward business ideas are not as simple as they first seem. It will be necessary for your c.e.d. organization to learn to assess how realistic its ideas for businesses are. In many cases, your organization will want to seek 'expert' assistance when evaluating the profit-making potential of a particular business. Different businesses will vary significantly in such areas as start-up costs, needs for working capital, time required to break-even, and advertising needs. However, it is very important to do some of the initial work yourselves, before bringing in outside help. It is also essential never to rely on only one set of opinions. Your assessment is a form of business investment. Good information, by helping you to avoid pitfalls and to maximize available opportunities, enhances the potential for your enterprise to be a success.

However, assessment is also expensive. The more time and money you spend on assessing, the less you have available for the business itself. Limit the time spent assessing each new project. Make every effort to gather relevant information, but do not expect to be able to find out everything. No new business is a sure thing. An element of risk is always involved. Community economic development organizations are usually involved in enterprises that the private sector considers too high-risk to be worthwhile. As a result, it is often necessary to proceed with a new project while many questions still remain unanswered. All that 'assessment' can do is to minimize some of the risks. Therefore, make constructive use of whatever information is available.

> When the Nimpkish Band acquired an old residential school building, several ideas for community projects became feasible. The physical assets of the building made it possible for the band council to experiment with some community businesses, with relatively little initial capital input.
>
> *"We got the building [the old residential school] and decided to start a café . . . no study, nothing, we just opened it. Then there was the lounge. It's been going three years now. It was no big deal, we just did it. We thought, if our people were going to drink, we might as well get the money to put into recreational programmes for the kids."*
> – Member, Nimpkish Band Council.

1. Collecting and Analyzing Community Information

Collecting the Information: Your first step will be to formally define your community. What are its geographic boundaries? Does it have interest-based boundaries as well? Next, you will want to gather relevant information concerning your community's past and present circumstances. You should be able to trace the development and growth of your community, not only in terms of events, but also in relation to certain statistics. Some of the information that is most commonly gathered includes:

a) *employment/unemployment figures* – relative to figures in other locations, as well as showing changes over time in your own community;
b) *average income levels* – relative to other regions, and whether incomes have been declining or increasing in your community over time;
c) *population figures;*
d) *education levels;*
e) *labour force characteristics* – identified by occupational category, amount of seasonal or part-time employment, and size of available work force within certain age categories;

f) *housing* – number of owners and tenants, standards, values and vacancy rates;
g) *local businesses and industries* – number and type;
h) *number of new businesses, bankruptcies and mergers;*
i) *amount of local investment by local banks in businesses;*
j) *number of job vacancies locally;*
k) *circulation of money* – new investments by year, indicators of circulation of capital, and indicators of consumer spending inside and outside your community; and
l) *external involvements*;
    i) government – local services, local jobs provided by public agencies, and local receipts of subsidies, grants and transfer payments;
    ii) private – outside ownership of local business, essential goods and services provided by external sources, and penetration of local markets by outside competitors with local businesses.

Analyzing the Data:

Analyze the data by dividing it into information relevant to local needs and local resources. This process is in many ways like the one we suggested for planning your project goals and activities. [Chapter 3]

a) Local Needs – a Sample

If your group is in agreement that some form of assistance for senior citizens is needed, but is undecided on whether to put its energies into organizing a drop-in centre (with recreational and social programmes), starting a 'visiting homemakers' service, or building apartments for senior citizens, the following information will be useful:

1. *Number of senior citizens in your community* – Is the number rising or falling, relative to the rest of the population? Is the number of senior citizens in your community above or below average?

The needs and interests of senior citizens vary from community to community.

2. *Income levels of senior citizens* – Is the average income higher or lower than the national average?

3. *Living conditions* – How many senior citizens live alone? How many are with families? How many people have moved outside your community to live because of a lack of suitable housing? How many are tenants? How many are owners? What are standards of housing like?

4. *Health* – How many are visited by nurses, health and social service workers, or local church members on a regular basis? How many are shut in? How many have a family doctor? How many have been in hospital in the last six months?

5. *Existing services* – e.g. nursing homes and programmes set up by local churches.

If incomes are low, then there will be a greater need for 'essential services' – those related to housing, nutrition and health care – as opposed to recreational programmes. If most people are in houses they own, as is true in many rural areas, they will tend to want services – like 'visiting home-makers' – that will allow them to stay in their homes for as long as possible. If they are tenants in the core area of a city, the greatest need may be for affordable lodgings that are in reasonably good condition. Often, local churches are active in organizing senior citizens' programmes. If your local churches are not active in this area, then there may be a great need for a drop-in centre to bring people together. And so on . . .

b) Analyzing Resources – Another Sample

If your group is considering starting a business like a firewood co-op, for example, the following information may be useful:

1. *Labour force* – How many people between the ages of 16 and 60 are listed as unemployed or seasonally unemployed? What proportion of the population is skilled, semi-skilled or unskilled?

2. *The wood resource* – What is the extent of the local wood resource? How much is unsuitable for commercial purposes like pulp and lumber? How much is on Crown Land? How much is on privately-owned wood lots? What is the state of health and maturity of the local wood resource?

3. *The fuel market* – How many people use wood for some portion of their domestic fuel needs? How does this compare with five years ago? Where is the nearest population centre? What proportion of homes there have fireplaces or wood stoves? Where are they presently getting their wood supply from?

4. *Other resources* – What are the capital and equipment needs of other firewood suppliers? What relevant skills do prospective co-op members have? What equipment is locally available for rent, lease, sale or exchange?

A combination of a seasonally employed labour force, small privately-owned wood lots or available Crown Land, an increase in the use of wood as a domestic fuel, and a core group of interested people who have skills, capital, equipment and/or access to wood lots, would indicate that the idea of a firewood co-op might be worth pursuing.

Most of this information can be obtained through Statistics Canada or through local municipal offices. Your Chamber of Commerce may have some business statistics. Your federal and provincial Members of Parliament can be helpful in directing you to government departments that have the kind of information you want, and in getting that information released for you. Research departments of political parties often have information that can be obtained through the offices of your local candidates. Also check with local libraries, educational institutions and other community organizations.

Always check and cite the date and source of information you are given. Watch carefully for information that is out of date, inaccurate, misleading or biased by the perspective of the group you receive it from.

2. Collecting and Analyzing Trade Information

Collecting the Information: You will be looking for standards to evaluate your ideas for projects against. The best sources are often people with experience in local industries, local banks or credit unions. They can tell you about the common problems, pitfalls and successes local businesses share. Those with experience directly related to your proposed venture can give you information about sources of supplies, markets, and legislation and regulations that will affect your project. You can also find out such information as: average profits, as a percentage of sales; average operating costs; average inventory needs; average mark-up on goods; and average cost of goods sold, based on the type of business and your projected level of sales.

There are several other potentially good sources of information:

1. Your Chamber of Commerce.

2. Your local planning office, which may have business maps showing locations and types of business activity.

3. Local libraries, colleges and universities.

4. Local banks, credit unions and financial institutions.

5. Government agencies, such as the Federal Business Development Bank, and departments of trade, commerce or economic development.

6. Many trade associations and business service organizations – e.g. Dun and Bradstreet – publish financial ratios for various businesses. These organizations often have research on the opportunities, problems and appropriate management strategies for different types of businesses.

7. Consultants, who specialize in starting small businesses or in a particular type of business. They will do original research for you. In addition, they can often give you previously prepared reports on the type of business you are considering. Remember that the viewpoint of most consultants

is not oriented to small-scale, community-owned, or not-for-profit businesses. Weigh their recommendations carefully, check them against other sources of information, and be prepared to reinterpret their findings to suit the special needs of community economic development. When conducting your search, there are a few things you should keep in mind:

1. Most studies, and people who work in government departments or educational institutions, will have a bias towards ideas and projects that are large in scale.

2. They will also presuppose that rapid and maximum expansion will be your goal.

3. Most community economic development projects are based on resources that have been ignored, because private entrepreneurs felt they were too small or would not generate a sufficient profit.

NUMBER OF INHABITANTS TO SUPPORT STORE
(by selected kinds of business)

National Averages

Kind of business	Number of inhabitants per store
Food stores	
Grocery stores, including delicatessens	770
Meat markets	11,463
Fish (seafood markets)	51,971
Fruit stores, vegetable markets	21,259
Candy, nut, confectionery stores	12,594
Dairy products stores	29,728
Bakery products stores	10,126
Eating, drinking places	
Eating places	842
Drinking places (alcoholic beverages)	1,705
General merchandise	
Department stores	44,379
Dry goods stores	34,152
General merchandise stores	6,899
Variety stores	8,430
Apparel, accessory stores	
Shoe stores	7,679
Women's clothing specialty stores	4,247
Children's infants-wear stores	33,057
Men's and boys' wear	8,403
Furniture, home furnishings, appliance dealers	
Furniture; home furnishings stores	3,437
Household appliances, radio, TV stores	6,148
Music stores, records and musical instruments	23,363
Automotive groups	
Passenger car dealers (franchised)	5,657
Passenger car dealers (non-franchised)	6,741
Tire, battery, accessory dealers	7,284
Aircraft, boat, motorcycle dealers	30,497
Household trailer dealers	46,456
Lumber, building materials, farm equipment dealers	
Farm equipment dealers	11,530
Lumber, building materials dealers	6,510
Paint, glass, wallpaper stores	16,239
Heating, plumbing, equipment dealers	40,589
Hardware stores	6,374
Drug stores, proprietary stores	
Drug stores	3,749
Proprietary stores	42,740
Other retail stores	
Fuel, ice dealers	7,559
Hay, grain, feed stores	13,547
Farm, garden supply stores	16,774
Jewelry stores	9,011
Book stores	59,815
Stationery stores	33,290
Sporting goods stores	17,270
Bicycle shops	100,083
Florists	9,527
Cigar stores, stands	38,509
News dealers, news stands	29,533
Gift, novelty, souvenir stores	14,965
Camera, photographic supply stores	57,030
Luggage, leather goods stores	140,684
Optical goods stores	14,792
Antique, secondhand stores	7,313
Hobby, toy stores	44,099
Pet shops	82,455

Source: Bureau of the Census, U.S. Department of Commerce.

Analyzing the Data: An important element of any project assessment – and the principal method you will use in analyzing your trade information – is a detailed market survey. A market survey answers many questions.

Market Analysis

Your customers:
- Who are they? Age, sex, income bracket.
- Where do they live, play, shop?
- What motivates them to buy your products?
- How often do they buy? Seasonal?
- Cash or credit?
- Can you afford to carry accounts receivable?

Your products:
- Are they unique, eye appealing?
- Better designed, higher quality?
- What sizes, any special packaging?
- Is there a need for your products?
- Must you offer a guarantee?
- What will be your return policy?
- Must you stock parts for service?

Distribution:
- If you are a manufacturer, how will you sell . . . through dealers, distributors, sales agents or direct to the consumer?
- What is common in the industry?
- Do transportation costs dictate the best method of distribution?

Advertising:
- How much is normal for your products?
- What media, how often? Seasonal?
- Do you have a logo or trademark? Is it registered?
- Is any free publicity available?
- Will you need an advertising agency?

† **Your competition:**
- How big, how old, how strong?
- What percentage of the market do they have?
- How far away?
- What advantages do you have?
- What advantages do they have?
- What percentage of the market will you get?

Buying:
- How much of each will you buy? From whom?
- Are you getting the best deal?
- Is volume discount eaten up by slow turnover?
- Can you return unsold merchandise?
- Have you a stock control plan to avoid overstocks, understocks and out of stocks?
- Have you established a line of credit with each supplier?
- How must you pay – C.O.D., 30 days, 60 days?

Pricing:
- Are your prices competitive?
- How important is low price?
- Is service more important?
- Must you give discounts for cash, volume, distributors, salesmen?
- What will discounts do to your mark-up?
- Must you include delivery cost in your price?

– W.F. Shave, *Starting a Small Business in Ontario*, 1978, pp. 3-4.

† Except in unusual circumstances, community economic development projects will not be starting new ventures that will compete directly with existing local businesses. Their purpose is to augment, not replace, the private sector.

3. Collecting and Using Financial Information

Collecting the Information: A crucial step in assessing a business idea is the collection of relevant financial information. This enables you to evaluate the profit-making potential of your proposed enterprise. Evaluating the financial viability of your new venture should give you answers to the following questions:

1. How much in assets – money and material goods – will your group need to start and maintain this business?

2. What are the costs associated with starting and maintaining your business? Which costs are fixed, and which will vary depending on the size and scope of your enterprise?

3. Where are you going to raise the money to start and maintain your business? What are your plans for obtaining loans, grants, sales, fees and share capital?

4. Under what conditions will you be able to raise the required capital?

5. Will you have money when you need it? How long will it take you to raise venture capital? How long will it be before you begin to receive revenues from your new business?

6. What strategies are available to you for dealing with the financial prolems – such as cash flow difficulties – that may arise?

7. When will the business break-even? When will it begin to make a profit?

Some of the information you need will be derived from your socio-economic data (e.g. sources of local investment funds), your trade information (e.g. the start-up costs of different types of businesses), and your market survey (e.g. whether you will need to extend credit to customers). The remainder will be determined by the financial situation of your own organization and the investment role it chooses for itself. Some community economic development projects take a debt position in new enterprises – i.e. they give loans to entrepreneurs. Others take an equity position – i.e. they take partial or total ownership in new enterprises. Relatively few Canadian community economic development projects have the necessary pool of capital to be able to provide debt financing. However, both approaches can be used with good results.

Using the Data: The information your organization compiles will enable it to describe and analyze the financial aspects of your business, using the following basic tools: the balance sheet; assessment of working capital; the income/operating statement; the break-even chart; and the cash flow statement.

a) The balance sheet One of the primary uses your information can be put to is in making up a balance sheet. Your balance sheet shows all the assets, liabilities and equity

BALANCE SHEET	
Date of Statement	
ASSETS	
Current	
Cash & Bank Accounts	
Stocks & Bonds at Cost (Mkt. Val. $)	
Cash Value Life Insurance	
Accounts Receivable (attach aged list)	
Less: Allowance for Doubtful	
Inventory at Lower of Cost or Market	
Prepaid Expenses	
Other Current Assets	
TOTAL CURRENT ASSETS (A)	
Fixed	
Land & Buildings	
Less: Accumulated Depreciation	
Furniture, Fixtures & Equipment	
Less: Accumulated Depreciation	
Automobiles	
Less: Accumulated Depreciation	
Leasehold Improvements – Net	
Other Assets	
TOTAL ASSETS	
LIABILITIES	
Current Debt	
Bank Loans	
Loans – Other	
Accounts Payable incl. Cheques in Transit	
Withholding and Sales Taxes Payable	
Income Taxes Payable	
Current Portion of Long-Term Debt	
Other Current Liabilities	
TOTAL CURRENT LIABILITIES (B)	
Long-Term Debt	
Mortgages & Liens Payable (attach details)	
Less: Current Portion	
Loans from Shareholders	
Other Loans of Long-Term Nature	
TOTAL LIABILITIES	
NET WORTH	
TOTAL LIABILITIES AND NET WORTH	
WORKING CAPITAL (A-B)	

as of a given date. The balance sheet is 'balanced' when the figures show that assets minus liabilities equal equity.

From your balance sheet, *you can calculate a current ratio* as follows:

$$\text{current ratio} = \frac{\text{current assets}}{\text{current liabilities}}$$

Current assets are those that are cash, or can easily be converted to cash within ninety days. Current liabilities are debts due within one year. Your banker will tell you that your current ratio is an indicator of your ability to pay off current debts. A ratio of two to one is considered the minimum indicator of sound financial status.

Your balance sheet also *allows you to calculate a quick ratio:*

$$\frac{\text{cash + accounts receivable}}{\text{current liabilities}}$$

This is another indicator of your ability to pay off current debts. If your ratio is one to one, you are probably in good shape.

Your equity ratio is:

$$\frac{\text{equity}}{\text{total assets}}$$

The relationship between the investment of your group in its enterprises and the total assets of the enterprises is often a significant factor in attracting private sector financing. Banks and credit unions like to see a ratio of 1:2, or 50%. Applications for loans or other forms of financing based on a low ratio are unlikely to be successful, unless they are very well-supported in other ways.

b) Assessment of working capital

Working capital, a source of many headaches for c.e.d. organizations, is also calculated from your balance sheet, as current assets minus current liabilities. Working capital is an indicator of the ease of cash flow – i.e. your ability to pay debts as they come due. The measure of adequate working capital varies greatly depending on your type of business, and such factors as amount of credit given, seasonal variation in your enterprise, and inventory needs. Trade associations or your bank/credit union can often provide you with information about typical ratios for your type of business.

c) The income/operating statement

Information from your accounts should also be summarized into an income statement. Your income statement shows income received and expenses incurred over a period of time. These are always prepared yearly, but can also be prepared weekly, monthly or quarterly as needed. The basic equation is income received minus expenses incurred equals net profit (before taxes). A comparison between actual and projected income, expenses and profits is often the starting point in making decisions about where and when to put energy into generating more income or cutting expenses. Many organizations make use of a work sheet. Work sheets are prepared – often on a monthly basis – to summarize all the financial transactions in a given period. Worksheets make it possible to make up balance sheets and income statements very quickly.

d) The break-even chart

The break-even chart is often useful for organizations that are relatively young enterprises. This chart divides expenses into fixed costs (such as rent, taxes and core salaries), and variable costs (expenses that change as incoming revenues change – e.g. cost of goods sold, advertising and promotion, and additional salaries). The chart shows the relationship between fixed costs, variable costs and total expenses at various levels of incoming revenue. It is particularly useful to retail or wholesale enterprises, where the variable costs change significantly depending on revenues (which are based on volume of sales). The break-even chart can be helpful in making budgeting decisions, plans for expansion, and in preparing business plans. Your accountant, and the trade information related to your specific type of business, can help you to estimate changes in your variable costs, typical profits at various levels of business, and other information you will need to construct a chart.

e) The cash flow statement

The cash flow statement compares projected cash receipts, outlays and balances with actual figures on a month by month basis. Estimates are usually prepared a year in advance. The idea is to try to minimize the cash flow problems that plague most small businesses by learning to anticipate in advance: where and when cash needs are greatest; and where and when extra cash is available that can be put to work in other ways – e.g. by being invested in new projects or placed in short-term, high interest savings accounts. Most c.e.d. organizations have little difficulty predicting expenses, but revenues – especially during the first few years – are more difficult to project.

BREAK-EVEN CHART

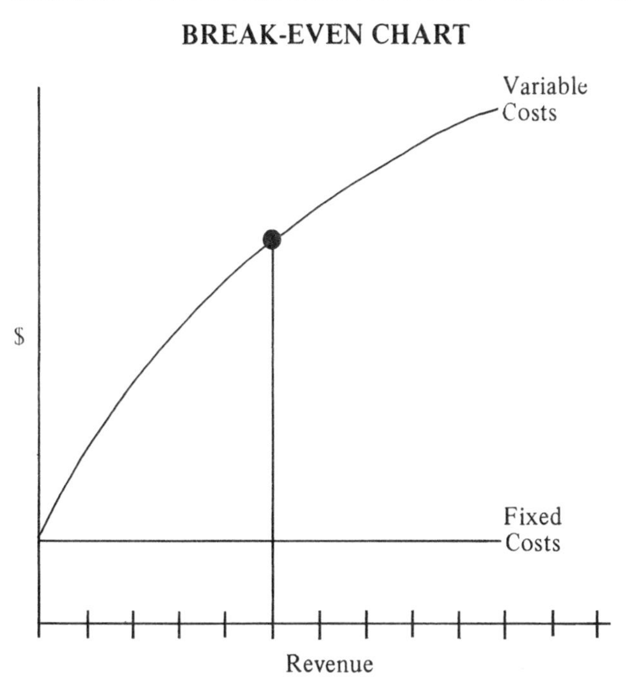

CASH FLOW
(Estimated Cash Forecast)

	Jan.	Feb.	Mar.
(1) Cash in Bank (Start of Month)			
(2) Petty Cash (Start of Month)			
(3) Total Cash (add 1 and 2)			
(4) Expected Cash Sales			
(5) Expected Collections			
(6) Other Money Expected			
(7) Total Receipts (add 4, 5 and 6)			
(8) Total Cash and Receipts (add 3 and 7)			
(9) All Disbursements (for month)			
*(10) Cash Balance at End of Month in Bank Account and Petty Cash (subtract (9) from (8))			

*This balance is your starting cash balance for the next month.

4. Writing Your Business Plan

The results of your venture assessment should be summarized into a business plan that includes:

a) information describing your organization;
b) the community or market area your organization is serving;
c) the people involved with the business idea; and
d) the finances of your business – present and future.

A Complete Business Plan Outline

1. Description and brief history of the business.
2. Number of employees by job category and current wage levels for each category.
3. Financial statements for the past three years: an income statement, a cash flow and a balance sheet.
4. Financial projections for the next three years: an income statement and a cash flow on a monthly basis for the first year and quarterly thereafter, and a balance sheet on a quarterly basis for the first year and annually thereafter.
5. Financial break-even analysis.
6. Amount of money required, and the uses to which it will be put.
7. Description of your product/service.
8. Markets for your product/service, including a list of major customers and the level of sales to each.
9. Names of your competitors and how you are able to meet the competition.
10. Names of your suppliers, including locations and amounts.
11. Management team, with resumes of principals.
12. Details of existing bank loans and capital of the company, including equity ownership and amounts invested.

– Massachusetts Community Development Finance Corporation, 2nd Annual Report, 1979, p.8.

Your business plan will normally include four types of financial forecasts:

1. Pro forma balance sheets prepared for: your start-up date; after your first six months; the end of the first year; and at the end of each of the next two years.†
2. When your business will begin to break-even.
3. When you expect to make a profit – profit and loss (income) statements for the next three years.
4. What your projections are for your cash flow needs for the next three years.

† A pro forma balance sheet is an estimated balance; it is used in projecting the financial situation of a new business.

Financial Management

Financial management involves generating money and making good use of it. We have already discussed the challenges involved in generating money: identifying projects with profit-making potential; locating and approaching outside funding sources; and managing projects well, in order to maximize their profit-making potential. The next few pages will focus on making good use of available funds.

1. Choosing from Investment Options

When a c.e.d. organization decides to invest in a profit-making enterprise, it has three basic options open to it: starting or buying a wholly-owned business; entering into a partnership, either as a full partner, a limited partner or as part of a co-operative arrangement; and buying a franchise.†

Wholly-owned Ventures:

Most groups start with a wholly-owned enterprise, and many limit themselves to this practice. There are a number of reasons for this. One is simplicity. For the average c.e.d. organization, with its limited capital resources and sources of management expertise, the added complications and risks of partnership with another group are intimidating. There is also a lack of suitable partners. In many situations, c.e.d. organizations are investing in high-risk ventures, and there is usually no other party around who not only has the money to invest, but is also willing to risk it on such chancy ventures.

Valley Woollen Mills is a wholly-owned venture of the Codroy Valley R.D.A.

† Community economic development organizations may also give loans, that is, take a 'debt' rather than an 'equity' investment position, e.g. CCEC Credit Union. However, most Canadian c.e.d. projects lack the continuing capital pool necessary to be able to offer loans as a regular service.

Partnerships: In many communities, there is a need to preserve and expand existing small businesses. A group that is well-established, with a pool of capital to invest and a credible record of past successes, can begin to offer – as one of its services – the exchange of capital or technical assistance for equity in other businesses. Contact and the N.C.E.A.S. are two community economic development projects that have chosen this approach. Usually a limited partnership is established when majority ownership and personal risk rest elsewhere; the c.e.d. organization's risks are limited to the amount of money invested.

Of course, community economic development organizations that provide capital and technical assistance in exchange for partial equity positions in other businesses have less control than they do over wholly-owned businesses. The danger, in addition to the financial risks assumed, is that the social and cultural goals of c.e.d. may be lost. In some cases, where the business itself serves a social or cultural need – e.g. a medical centre or a craft co-op – this danger is less. Often the benefits accrued by preserving a community's small businesses outweight the apparent dangers. Each organization makes its own decision about how best to invest its money in order to reach its goals.

Co-operatives – Full Partnerships: We have not heard of examples in Canada of the full partnership type of investment – i.e. where a c.e.d. organization shares all the risks of the business with one or more partners. The co-operative arrangement, where a c.e.d. organization joins a co-op as a member, is more common. CCEC, for example, has over 100 member organizations, some of which are c.e.d. organizations themselves. However, it seems likely that as c.e.d. organizations in Canada mature, they will begin to explore available partnership options more fully.

Franchises: A franchise is a form of business contract. It is a business agreement that allows one party (the franchisee), to sell a particular product or service within a specified territory and in a specified way. The product or service is usually identified by symbols, such as trade names, logos, elements or store design, that are wholly-owned by the franchisor. For example, many fast food restaurants or corner store chains are franchises; and independent salesmen, advertising 'exclusive lines' of cars, cosmetics or whatever, are often part of the franchise system as well.

When you purchase a franchise, you are purchasing a proven product or service – plus other benefits that may be written into your contract, such as marketing assistance, managerial training and proven operating methods. In return, the franchisor gets your purchase fee, and sometimes royalties or service charges based on your profits. Your contract will also bind you to exclusive use of your franchisor as supplier of various materials and goods you will need to use in your business.

Franchises can be attractive to c.e.d. groups, if they can find a franchise that is consistent with their goals. For inexperienced business people, a good franchise will help diminish some of the risks of starting a business – it can also return a substantial profit. The disadvantages of franchises vary, depending on the contract. Some franchises are nothing more than devices used to steal money from the unsuspecting. Others have such tight contracts, that the ability of the franchisee to adjust his/her business to local conditions may be virtually non-existent.

If your organization decides to consider a franchise, check it out with the utmost care. Talk to your lawyer, your accountant, the Better Business Bureau and at least one established franchisee. Consider all the possible implications of every term in the contract before your group signs.

2. Bookkeeping

Whatever type of investment you choose, a good bookkeeping system is essential to making effective use of your money. Your books not only allow you to monitor the financial health of your organization on a daily, weekly, monthly or yearly basis, but also provide essential planning information. From the information in your books, you can project your future financial needs and your available resources for expanding, improving or starting new projects.

Bookkeeping is not difficult; neither is it time-consuming relative to its value to your organization. The amount of time it takes varies with the size and complexity of your organization. In organizations involved in only one or two profit-making enterprises, bookkeeping will take up less than one hour out of the day. The elements of a good bookkeeping system are available to every community economic development organization. All you need is:

1. A means of recording and keeping original information in files – e.g. bank statements, cancelled cheques, receipts and invoices.

2. Some accounts or ledgers – recorded on cards, in separate books or on separate pages in a book – where transactions can be recorded as they occur.

3. A journal – a general book in which all transactions from the accounts or ledgers are listed.

4. A specific time set aside for regular bookkeeping.

The secret to good bookkeeping is regularity. All financial transactions should be recorded on the day they occur. Every day, time should be set aside for bookkeeping. Neglect very quickly leads to chaos – not only with respect to your records, but also with respect to your ability to make good decisions about handling the finances of your organization. Neglect of bookkeeping will also result in unpleasant and costly meetings with your accountant, who will be forced to increase his or her fee in direct relation to the amount of time spent in trying to sort out the confusion caused by sloppy or irregular bookkeeping.

The best approach is to start off by setting up a very simple double-entry bookkeeping system. The system can be adapted or altered as need be. Although many large corporations now have computerized systems, they are neither affordable nor necessary for most c.e.d. organizations. The traditional hand-recorded system still works very well and is usually the most efficient, even for large and complex c.e.d. groups.

Every bookkeeping system – simple or complex – is based on five different sets of accounts:
a) *assets* – what is owned;
b) *liabilities* – what is owed;

c) *equity* – the investment of the owners;
d) *revenues* – money generated by the organization; and
e) *expenses* – costs of running the enterprise.

The following information is entered into those accounts:

1. Cash on hand or in the bank – a record of all cash received, where it came from and where it went.

2. Accounts receivable – you need records of all money owed to your business, who owes it, what arrangements for payment have been made, balances owed, and payments made or overdue.

3. Inventory – if your enterprise is a retail or wholesale business, you will be carrying inventory. Its value is usually calculated from the lowest cost of production or market value.

4. Other assets – buildings, land, machinery and equipment – should all be recorded at the value they had when purchased. All of these assets, except land, depreciate yearly. The amount of depreciation is calculated on an estimate of the number of years the asset will last. A percentage of the value of the asset is subtracted each year, so that at the end of the estimated life of an asset, the book value is zero.

5. Accounts payable – all debts owed, to whom, for how much, when payments are due, what payments have been made, and what balance is due.

6. Payroll – all salaries, wages, deductions and cheques issued must be recorded.

7. Taxes.

8. Operating expenses – costs incurred, divided into relevant categories (e.g. in manufacturing firms, costs are divided into production costs, selling costs and administrative costs).

9. Purchases made.

Procedures for gathering this information can be built right into the operation of your business. Your accountant and books on accounting can advise you. *The basic rule is to ensure that every transaction is recorded* – e.g. on a cash register tape, in a cheque book, on an invoice, receipt, inventory slip or payroll sheet. You should be able to trace every 'entry' – i.e. keep all those slips of paper in files until your accountant tells you that you can throw them away.

3. Annual Reports

Every community-based organization should produce an annual report that includes a report of its financial status. Depending on your legal structure, you may be legally required to produce an audited statement. Legal requirements aside, however, if a community organization is to be truly accountable to the community it represents, then it must be able to make financial information available on a yearly basis. It is your accountant's job to help you. S/he will compare information in your files with your journal entries and records of accounts. If you have worksheets, these too will be checked against the journal, records of accounts or ledger entries. From this validated information, your accountant prepares year-end balance sheets, income statements, and other statements as required.

Most accountants are happy to have you consult with them when you first set up your books. They can help you to devise a simple and useful system that will be workable for everyone. Most accountants do not mind occasional enquiries about how various bookkeeping entries should be made. They are happy to answer occasional enquiries because it helps to avoid the 'accountants' nightmare' – being presented with a large cardboard carton of 'papers' shortly before income tax time.

Most c.e.d. organizations sail 'close to the wind'. Profits are never great. As a result, careful and conscientious attention to finances is of critical importance. Problems that are ignored or not identified may quickly become insoluble.

For Further Reading:

Archer M., White, J., **Starting and Managing Your Own Small Business**, Toronto, *Financial Post,* 1979.

Cornish, Clive, C.G.A., **Our Accountant's Guide to Running a Small Business**, Vancouver, Self-Counsel Press, 1953.

Federal Business Development Bank, Ottawa, publishes *Minding Your Own Business,* a series of pamphlets on various aspects of starting and managing small businesses. Offices in most cities in Canada.

Husack, G.A., Gibbons, R.W., **A Feasibility Study for New Service Ventures**, Kitchener, Ontario, The Institute for Small Business, 1979.

Institute for New Enterprise Development, Cambridge, Mass., publishes a variety of materials useful to organizations involved in community economic development. See especially, *How to Prepare a Business Plan*.

James, J.D., **Starting a Successful Business in Canada**, Vancouver, International Self-Counsel Press, 4th ed., 1978.

Ministry of Culture and Recreation (Ontario) *Bookkeeping procedures for community groups*, Toronto, 1976.

Shave, W.F. for Ministry of Industry and Tourism (Toronto), **Starting a Small Business in Ontario**, Toronto, 1978.

7

Managing Your Organization

The issues relating to new organizations and new projects that we have discussed so far in **Community Profit** *are also very much a part of the ongoing life of your organization. However, the management of established organizations requires attention being paid to some important additional factors. This chapter discusses some of the things that are essential to keeping your organization running smoothly.*

The People in Your Organization

The 'people' part of any successful c.e.d. project is based on an inherent respect for their worth and dignity. This is not to say that c.e.d. organizations should allow themselves to be trampled upon by the greedy, selfish or corrupt. Your organization cannot be managed with the expectation that theft or manipulation will never take place. However, honest and empathetic management practices can minimize the chances of such occurrences ever happening. Whatever structure you chose for your c.e.d. project, the way in which your organization actually functions will be determined by the people who are its members.

> *"I think there would be several of us who just wouldn't let go [of this project], unless it was just dismal. We'd go looking for other money . . ."*
> – Employee, Comfort Clothing Services.

Roles People Play

Initially, c.e.d. organizations (usually) include two identifiable groups of people: a board of directors and general members. All are volunteers. Later, staff members may be added; and volunteers who are not members, but who work with your organization. Of course, all these 'categories' are not mutually exclusive. We have already mentioned how volunteers often develop into staff members. It is not unusual, either, for employees to sit on the board as directors. Although overlap is common, everyone has a specific role to play in your organization. Much of the tension and conflict in c.e.d. groups is generated because of confusion about roles and responsibilities.

1. Members

> *"Our group is perhaps better than most, but we've got all the traditional problems of any group. We've got doers and shirkers . . ."*
> – Member, Mira Pasture Co-op.

"It's true in any organization that it's run by a small group – they push the thing. You have to make them answerable to the large group, build that in. They can't be too 'expert', too divorced from the rest. There's a tendency for that to happen in a co-op. Every co-op is like that . . ."
– Member, Mira Pasture Co-op.

The reality of any organization is that it is divided into three kinds of members:

1. A small active core group that is never large in relation to the total size of the membership.

2. An interested membership that can always be called upon in an emergency, and when asked, will usually be more than willing to help out. These people do not want positions of 'responsibility', but they do have a genuine interest in participating. They are the ones who, as things evolve, will sometimes become more involved. They represent the primary source of new leadership for your organization.

3. 'Shadow members', who express an interest in participating, but who somehow never do. The barriers to active participation may have nothing to do with your organization – such things as sickness or problems at home, that could not have been anticipated when the member first 'signed up'. Or, the person may be uncertain of his or her ability and/or desire to participate. The best approach with your shadow members is to try to avoid being too critical of them, but not to spend much time trying to involve them, unless they ask for assistance.

Recognition: All members have one primary need in common – recognition for the work they do. In c.e.d. organizations, where the contribution of volunteers is often critical to the success of the organization, it is essential to acknowledge their importance. Often the small courtesies will mean the most to volunteers: a note or a phone call to say thank you on behalf of everyone; or public recognition at a meeting or in a local newspaper. In c.e.d. organizations, where people are often very busy, it is difficult to take the time to always be stopping to say 'thank you'. Recognition, however, is part of the basic respect for people and abilities that is one of the philosophical bases of community economic development. It is a principle that cannot be neglected.

Board Members: Almost every c.e.d. organization has voluntary help in one critical part of its structure – the board of directors. Board members can bring the following elements to your organization: they can be representative of the varying interests, skills, expertise and contacts in your community; and they can represent the particular needs of your organization at the community level. In general, organizations select board members who are trustworthy, likeable and will provide the above.

Boards of c.e.d. organizations are active and play a number of essential roles:
a) they set priorities, goals and objectives for the organization;
b) they establish criteria used to evaluate ideas for new projects, both non-profit and for-profit;
c) they make the final decision on new ventures and projects;
d) they participate in hiring and firing staff;
e) they report back to other community members;
f) they bring to the c.e.d. organization the feelings and ideas of various community people;
g) they offer skills, expertise, and contacts with other people who may have skills, expertise and knowledge to offer; and
h) they help to recruit new members for your organization.

a) Selecting your board

New board members can be elected or appointed, either by the other board members or by the wider membership of your group. Often the best approach is for board members to elect or appoint new members, based on criteria adopted by the wider membership. This is not only a simple approach; it also helps to ensure that new board members feel welcomed by other members. The group then has a better chance of being able to function as a cohesive unit.

Groups often face the difficulty of wanting their boards to include: business and professional people with important skills and knowledge, and potentially useful contacts; and representatives of the sectors of the community that the organization wishes to serve – e.g. youth, the unemployed and low-income people. Such different types of people will not always be able to work together effectively. Business and professional people often carry with them an aura of self-confidence, education, skill and wealth that can be very intimidating. They are also used to working in situations where it is important to be aggressive, assertive and efficient. Conversely, people from other sectors of the community are often more used to social gatherings and informal meetings. They may never have encountered business and professional people before, except as customers – or opponents.

Having a 'mixed' board is never easy. Fortunately, the two basic requirements for making it work – honesty and understanding – are not complex. These things are available to everyone. However, the task of bringing that honesty out and developing that understanding can be difficult. It usually requires a great deal of forethought and sensitivity.

b) Learning to Work Together

Given time, most business and professional people can learn to talk simply and clearly, and to operate in a more 'sociable' manner in meetings. People from the rest of the community, for their part, learn the ins and outs of how to organize and run meetings, and to take on previously unfamiliar roles, such as chairing. Eventually, any feelings of intimidation usually pass, as people become more willing to speak their minds. At Comfort Clothing, for example, the board was initially made up of volunteers from Kingston's business and professional communities. Since then, not only has employee representation on the board been increasing every year, but so has the number of employee representatives who hold executive positions. This year, in fact, all executive positions on the board have been filled by employee representatives for the first time.

"Well, when you really get down to it, it's a matter of trust . . ."
– Member, East York Recycling.

The ability of your Board to work as a group is very important. Board members need to be able to get along well together – to respect and like one another. They will also need to trust one another. Your board will handle many issues (like hiring, firing, and accepting or rejecting ideas for new projects), that require confidentiality and integrity. If your board members are unwilling to discuss issues openly with one another for fear that information will be mishandled in some way, they will be unable to work together effectively.

c) Using a co-ordinator/chairperson

However, this learning process does take time. It requires sympathetic and honest work by a chairperson, co-ordinator or manager, if the business/professional representatives are not to become impatient and take over, leaving other members in a situation where the most attractive option is to drop out.

d) Using advisory committees

Some groups deal with this type of problem by placing all the business/professional people on a special 'advisory committee' to the board, allowing the board itself to be a more homogeneous group. In situations where there is no one with the skills to balance the varying needs of different board members, this may be the best option. In most cases, though, the benefits that people bring to the board are far greater if they are given the status of full members. Like other members of your organization, they have a strong need for recognition. The other benefit of a 'blended' board is that it represents a straightforward approach to a problem that must eventually be faced anyway – i.e. board members of all types have to learn to work together, whether or not they are divided into separate committees.

e) Board size

Your board needs to be large enough in size to spread the work around. Board members are volunteers and cannot be expected to devote all their time to your organization. You need enough board members to be able to accomplish you board's workload within reasonable time limits. Your board should not be too large. Ten is often the optimum number. If your board has more than twelve members, it will be essential to have an executive committee to act as a co-ordinating body. Otherwise, effective management becomes very difficult. The exact number of board members will depend on the needs of your organization. Groups we visited had boards with from three to eighteen members.

Volunteers:

"The Credit Union can always use more volunteers and we'd have trouble maintaining our level of operation as it now stands without them. If you have some financial or office skills and would like to donate some time, please get in touch with us."
– CCEC Credit Union brochure.

"We expect our group members to do work – members donated a lot of equipment and their labour too . . . Some people give more than others. We discussed a quota, but it's never been formalized yet."
– Member, Mira Pasture Co-op.

Organizations differ greatly in their approach to the use of volunteer assistance. Some, like the Mira Pasture Co-op, depend on the voluntary work of their members to accomplish the day-to-day business of their organization. Others, like Comfort Clothing, do not have voluntary workers except for the board members. In the early years of most c.e.d. projects, there is little or no money for salaries. As a result, volunteers fill all positions – directors, managers and workers. Later, when revenues become available to pay staff, the situation changes. There seems to be a natural tendency for voluntary input at the staffing level to gradually fall off, as the paid workers take on more and more work (later in this section, we discuss how to fight this tendency).

Some organizations incorporate voluntary work into their enterprises in an informal way – e.g. Is Five's East York Recycling Project. People participate voluntarily in the project and receive no direct return, other than the knowledge that their 'garbage' is being recycled. They make their voluntary contribution by: washing and separating out glass and tin; collecting and tying newspapers and cardboard; and placing these things out for pick-up. Although the total amount of effort on the part of each participant is not large, it is significant, since the recycling project could not exist without them. Non-profit craft shops (that operate on a consignment basis), and second-hand clothing exchanges are examples of voluntary co-operative businesses.

> *"The wives of most of the men are tremendously interested in this project and do a lot for us. These women are terrific, terrific support. They really encourage the thing. One woman does all our phoning for meetings. I've said that I think the men should do their own phoning, but she says she wants to do it. It's something she can do and still be be getting her work done at home."*
> – Member, Mira Pasture Co-op.

Probably the most common use of voluntary help – after board participation – is that made on a temporary or ad hoc advisory basis. Many groups, when a new idea is suggested, establish a working committee to examine its feasibility. The committee usually consists of one or more board members, and may include a staff member. Other people with specific expertise are also recruited; their job is to advise on the feasibility of the idea. Alternatively, groups may not form committees, but will approach people individually to ask for their reactions to a new idea. This kind of 'short-term loan' of expertise not only represents a very valuable asset for c.e.d. organizations; it is often a very convenient arrangement for everyone concerned.

a) Using volunteers effectively

As an organization matures and grows more complex, it is more and more difficult to make a place for volunteers. Besides the need for recognition that we have already referred to, volunteers require: a thorough introduction to all parts of your organization; lots of ongoing support and assistance; work to do that they enjoy; and a means of keeping in touch with what is going on throughout your organization. Recruiting, co-ordinating and managing volunteer staff is a big job. Most groups have difficulty fitting it in.

"It's not an easy organization to fit into – people here tend to be very self-sufficient and independent . . . I could have used more supervision, especially at first. I think we sometimes forget what it must be like to be where we all were five years ago . . . I think we've sometimes been a bit impatient with new people."
– Volunteer, Is Five Foundation.

Groups that do have a large corps of volunteer workers usually operate some sort of 'buddy system', whereby an already experienced individual takes on the responsibility of integrating a new volunteer into the 'life' of the organization.

Staff:

"A good manager is someone who can stay on top of everything, who is willing to listen to the problems of everybody."
– Member, Nimpkish Band Council.

"Get somebody who works hard and is good with people . . ."
– Member, Mira Pasture Co-op.

The community economic development organization that has been fortunate enough to generate funds to hire staff, is able to significantly increase its workload. However, hiring staff also introduces a whole new set of problems, such as:
a) how to hire;
b) what to look for in a staff person;
c) whether to hire locally or from outside the community;
d) salaries and wages – i.e. how to pay people;
e) personnel policies – i.e. what is important; and
f) how having paid staff will alter the way the organization works.

There are no easy answers to any of these questions. In some cases, other non-profit organizations can give you the benefit of their experiences. In others, you will have to make a decision based solely on your board's consensus of what is likely to work best.

a) How to hire

Hiring can be tricky, especially in small communities where work is not plentiful. It is important, regardless of the size of the community, to establish a hiring process, write it down, and stick to it. However, in situations – e.g. the Mira Community Pasture – where a volunteer position grows into a paid one, it is usually only necessary to have the minutes of the meeting in which the decision was made.

When there is a competition for a position, a more complicated process is necessary. Some groups have found that it adds credibility and legitimacy to their efforts to ask all applicants to register with 'Manpower' and be referred from the local Canada Employment Centre. In fact, when salaries are coming out of government grants, this is usually required. Remember to specify the date all applications are due by, when you are posting advertisements or making arrangements with Manpower.

STAFF OPENINGS AT THE IS FIVE DOWNTOWN OFFICE

Office Manager: Is Five requires a full-time secretary to perform receptionist, bookkeeper, typist, and general support roles. Applicants should be self-starters with relevant technical skills and knowledge of environmental issues. A fair "community" salary will be paid. Contact: JoAnne Opperman, 531-3548.

Also,

Committee Assistant: A Toronto volunteer recycling group, with which Is Five is affiliated, requires a part-time paid assistant to carry out public relations and research. Applicants should be assertive, have relevant technical skills, and be familiar with solid waste issues. This is a contract position with an office location in downtown Toronto. Contact: c/o JoAnne Opperman, 531-3548.

Marketing Manager: The R.C.O. requires a recyclable materials salesperson. Applicants should be assertive, possess keen negotiating skills, and have familiarity with solid waste issues. A fair "community" salary will be paid. Contact: Eric Hellman, 533-6757.

Executive Assistant: The R.C.O. requires an assistant to the Director. Applicants should have knowledge of solid waste issues, research experience, written and spoken communication skills, creativity, organizing ability, and capability for working long, flexible hours under informal conditions. A fair "community" salary will be paid. Contact: Eric Hellman, 533-6757.

– Is Five Foundation, *Another Newsletter,* June 1979.

The next step is to appoint one or two people (board and/or other staff members), to look through the applications and pick out the ones that come closest to the established criteria. This 'short list' is then passed on to another committee – e.g. the whole board – for approval, before interviewing takes place. The best approach is to interview by committee. Sometimes prospective employees are interviewed twice: once during a tour of ongoing activities; and once, somewhere where uninterrupted conversation can take place. Remember that it is also important for the applicant to have an opportunity to interview your group.

Members of your organization – regardless of status – should be able to participate in the hiring process. Their ability to get along with a new staff member is essential to the success of your organization. However, the final decision must be made by the members of your board. Sometimes, everything up until final board approval is handled by staff, but it is generally better to have some board members involved in the process from start to finish. Not only does this provide additional opinions, but it also helps to keep board members in touch with the day-to-day workings of your organization.

b) What to look for

The criteria that you judge your applicants by should be based on four factors: interpersonal, technical and organizational competence, and commitment. Commitment to the concept of c.e.d. is always important, but the relative importance attached to each of these factors will depend on the position you are hiring for, and the other resources available to you. Hiring a manager often poses the biggest problem, since 'everything' is essential. Your manager needs: to be able to get along well with a wide variety of people – staff, board members, volunteers, and clients or customers; to be able to plan and organize in consultation with others; to know how to successfully run non-profit enterprises; and to be committed to the idea of community-controlled economic development. In addition, managers – like everyone else – must possess the honesty, integrity and respect for others that the philosophy of c.e.d. demands.

People with that particular combination of skills and ideals are not plentiful. The need to have a manager 'in place' forces some groups to hire people who are not fully qualified. This can be damaging to your organization, unless you take steps to provide a new manager with the skills s/he needs as quickly as possible. Groups we visited indicated that 'technical competence' was the most difficult requirement to locate. Canada, unlike the United States, does not have an 'entrepreneurial class' to draw from. It is very hard to find people who have expertise in starting and running various kinds of businesses. As a result, not only do groups have trouble finding technically skilled managers, but they also have trouble finding sources of good technical training and assistance. Many c.e.d. organizations end up learning the job on a trial and error basis. Although learning through 'on-the-job' experience is good, the trial and error approach can easily result in serious financial losses and poor morale. At present, this is one of the biggest problems facing c.e.d. organizations.

In order to find the necessary degree of technical competence, Contact has hired some managers from 'outside' the immediate community. The greenhouse manager is a university graduate from another part of the region.

c) Where to look

Hiring criteria usually have priority over automatically staffing from within the community. It is always preferable, however, to hire locally. The dilemma arises when those conditions do not exist – i.e. should a local person without the required skills be hired, or an outsider with those necessary skills? In general, when an organization is young, with little staff and few training resources – and with the local community watching carefully for signs of success or failure – the best approach is to hire the most skilled person. If this person is an 'outsider', there may be some 'community backlash'. At this stage, it is more important to establish the 'legitimacy' that success brings. Later, when your organization has begun to prove itself to the community and you have a core of experienced people, every effort should be made to hire locally – even if you have to hire people without the necessary skills.

Any 'outsider' brought in needs to be treated with sensitivity and consideration. To be from somewhere else is never easy, especially in a community organization. It is very important to take the time to introduce a new person to the way things are done, not only in your organization, but also in your community – and to be frank about the possibility of 'community backlash'.

d) Wages and salaries

Most c.e.d. organizations operate with a 'flattened' salary system. The range between the upper and lower ends of the wage scale are not as far apart as in many other organizations. Most c.e.d. organizations have a stated commitment to paying people what they are worth, but are unable financially to match private or public sector wages for management positions. They also have a stated commitment to providing a 'living wage' – i.e. paying people enough so that they can make ends meet. Hence, the relatively high wages for normally low-paying jobs, and low wages for high-paying jobs. The concept of a 'fair community wage', as something that is adequate but is not competitive, is becoming quite common.

The idea of paying for good quality work is directly linked to the c.e.d. philosophy – i.e. that every person should be treated with respect. When there is little money available for wages, it is often better to hire part-time at a fair wage, than full-time at a poor rate. The former can generally contribute as much as – or more than – the latter.

e) Personnel policies

In small organizations, the working environment is shaped by personal relationships. Therefore, it is particularly important to have stated personnel policies right from the beginning. Your organization will need policies in the following areas, as soon as it has hired its first employees:
a) wages and salary scales;
b) vacations;
c) sick leave;
d) leaves of absence;
e) working conditions;
f) safety;
g) promotions and raises; and
h) hiring and firing.

Although many small businesses operate without written personnel policies, most well-established c.e.d. organizations have developed manuals on personnel policies, and systems for keeping personnel records. Your records for every employee should include:

a) *personal information*, such as letters or documents submitted during hiring, or material relating to performance evaluation;
b) *employment records*, showing date of hiring, changes in status, etc.;
c) *payroll records*; and
d) *a job description*.

Be sure to consult your accountant about your organization's obligations as an employer. Contributions to C.P.P. and U.I.C. have to be made. You may also want to look into optional benefits, such as group health insurance and life insurance. The advice of other organizations can be very useful when making these decisions . As a good 'community' employer, your organization should try to offer its employees a reasonable benefits package. Remember, however, that each 'benefit' is an added cost to your organization. Some organizations start off by offering only those benefits required by law, and add to their 'packages' when they can afford to. This is obviously not the best solution, but it may be the only practical one.

f) Developing board/staff relationships

"I feel this is a big danger – the only way you can overcome this is by having frequent meetings of the whole group. You have to consult with them and make them realize they're making the decisions and you are carrying them out."
– Member, Mira Pasture Co-op Executive.

"Often we give directions to the Board of Directors – it's the only way it can work."
– CCEC staff member.

When you add staff to an organization, you are altering it in a significant way. A typical pattern is that over time, more and more tasks are taken on by the staff. Volunteer assistance falls off and the board becomes less active – i.e. approving rather than making decisions. It is very important to guard against this, because sooner or later the power of the staff will begin to be resented; and/or the staff will come to feel isolated and overburdened.

Clearly defined roles for board, staff and other volunteers are essential. Job descriptions are always a good idea. In general, the responsibility of staff members is to ensure that your c.e.d. organization functions smoothly on a day-to-day basis. Technical decisions are usually staff decisions, while broader policy matters are the responsibility of the board. Staff and board members share a responsibility for co-ordinating their relationship: they need to devise a way of working that keeps board members up-to-date, involved and ready to advise when appropriate.

The exact nature of the board/staff working relationship differs with each group. Often it is helpful to sit down and work out the details of the relationship by using a series of examples. Whatever the details, the relationship must be based on honesty, mutual respect and a shared understanding of the importance of working together. Board and staff members must like one another and be able to get along together. This congeniality is as essential to the selection of staff or board members, as any degree of status or technical competence.

Developing a 'Learning Organization'

"Even if training is part of your programme, the work experience has to be practical."
– Employee, Comfort Clothing Services.

"The more people can handle by themselves the better – it's what keeps people here."
– Member, East York Recycling.

". . . it is more productive and a better use of resources, to increase the authentic participation of employees in the running of organizations."
– CCEC Credit Union Newsletter, November 1979.

People in c.e.d. organizations generally work long hours for little or no pay. It is typical for these organizations to operate on a 'shoe-string', so people have to make do without things like modern offices and furnishings, useful equipment, free coffee, company cars and free conferences. When we talked to people across the country about working conditions in c.e.d. organizations, their responses were very similar. They stay for two reasons: one is their commitment – i.e. their desire to see the organization succeed; and the other is that c.e.d. organizations allow them to continue to learn new skills in a unique working situation.

The opportunities to confront new problems, to take on new responsibilities, and to learn new skills are crucial factors in compensating for some of the disadvantages of working for a c.e.d. organization. Every organization needs to build this opportunity into their structure. Opportunities exist through: job-sharing; movement from one position to another; or taking on new projects. Equally important are other training opportunities – courses, conferences and workshops.

"It's a factory, like any other. It's noisy and dusty and sometimes it's cold. And you're on your feet all day. But it's a job. It's good for me – fits with my family. I can be home in time to make the kids their evening meal. If there's a storm or you're sick, they take it into account. And it's a good group to work with. We're a small place . . . It's a good job for me."
– Employee, Valley Woollen Mills.

1. Working Together

Community economic development groups recognize the importance of a supportive environment. They work hard to develop and maintain a high level of open, honest communication and mutual respect.

*"I didn't want to work for someone, and didn't like it the other way around either . . . The concept I was most attracted to was **working with people.**"*
– Member, Is Five Foundation.

"We kid each other a lot . . . have a lot of fun. We also want people to speak their mind."
– Member, Mira Pasture Co-op.

A good understanding of communications and a mastery of effective decision-making are essential to the development of a healthy working environment.

When skills are less than adequate or problems have developed, training programmes for staff, board members and other volunteers can be very helpful.*

2. Communications

The people interviewed for this book stressed the need for organizations that permitted members to participate and kept them informed.

> *"You [board members] can't run too far ahead. You only cause alienation. You have to continually check yourself – is everyone on board, is the group on track?"*
> – Member, Is Five Foundation.

At Is Five, and at other community economic development organizations, the kind of organization needed to allow for good communications changed as the organization grew. Periodic re-evaluation has been necessary.

> *"We have a communications problem – everyone is so busy on their own projects. It's hard to get everyone involved, informed. We need more structure now."*
> – Member, Is Five Foundation.

A good communications system is one where: people feel comfortable talking to one another; information is available to anyone who wants it and is directly affected by it; and decision-makers are striving to get ideas and suggestions from as many people as possible, and are integrating them into their plans.

Internal Communications:

> *"Our membership is kept in touch. We have regular meetings and we talk on the phone."*
> – Member, Mira Pasture Co-op.

Most c.e.d. groups are small, so the task of keeping everyone involved and informed can be managed without much difficulty. Regular staff/volunteer meetings, review sessions and social gatherings, like a potluck dinner, are popular methods of bringing people together to share information and discuss issues. When time is limited and/or it is impossible to get everyone together, a report posted on the notice board, an open memo circulated throughout the organization, or a newsletter to every member can be an effective means of keeping people in touch.

Communications with Your Community:

Early in a c.e.d.'s history a decision has to be made, regarding whether your project should have a high or a low profile. This decision will affect how your c.e.d. group communicates with the community. Projects, which are trying to keep a low profile, usually keep their communities informed, and solicit reactions to their activities through board members and other volunteers. Board members often belong to several community organizations, and can easily channel information or 'check things out' for the project. If members decide that a high profile in the community is necessary, or an issue arises that should be brought to the attention of the entire community, more public methods are used: general newsletters; public meetings; articles in newspapers or magazines; or interviews on newscasts or public affairs shows. The Codroy Valley Woollen Mill, for example, announced its opening via an article that was published in a magazine sold throughout all of eastern Canada.

> *"New Dawn is not a co-operative, where members take part in a democratic decision-making process. Still, the main thrust of the organization requires that a continuous assessment of needs of the community be made, since these provide areas within which New Dawn might act; also it requires a certain degree of social control since, as a non-profit community based enterprise, New Dawn purportedly caters to the needs of the community. The way in which these community inputs and controls are provided, however, has to be compatible with the efficient management of a business enterprise, requiring continuity and speed in decision-making."*
> – J. Hanratty ed., *New Dawn Enterprises Limited*, Technical Bulletin No. 7, Revised 1979, p. 54.

3. Decision-making

How decisions should be made and who should make them is a crucial question for any community economic development project. All projects strive to be democratic. How they achieve democracy varies. The age and size of the group, its specific philosophy towards work, the cultural background of its members, and the priorities the group has set for itself, all influence its approach to decision-making.

Models of Decision-making:

a) The collective – consensus

Groups which are small and just beginning often rely on decisions by consensus. A slow process, but an effective one, it can build a strong and very committed group. CCEC staff work this way. All decisions dealing with the daily functioning of the office are discussed by the three staff members. Discussion continues until a solution that is agreeable to all parties has been suggested.

b) The centralized model – modified consensus

Once a project reaches the point where it is sponsoring several activities and its membership has increased, most community economic development groups change their approach in the interests of efficiency. This can work in several ways. One of CCEC's staff members described it as 'living in a co-operative house' – there are private areas and public areas. Each person takes full responsibility for managing his or her private area, following rules set by all members of the house. All members participate in decision-making about the 'public areas'. In community economic development groups, 'public areas' are often such issues as new projects, personnel policies and use of office space.

Is Five has adopted a system which one of its members calls 'centralized democracy'. Simply put, this approach stresses maximizing the delegation of authority to individual workers, and encouraging members to discuss problems and put forward suggestions to the board of directors. Final decisions are left to the members of the board.

c) The co-operative – one member/one vote

The Mira Community Pasture is organized as a co-operative. In addition to the general membership, there is an elected executive and a manager. The executive co-ordinates the group's activities and acts as a spokesman for the group, while the manager is responsible for the day-to-day activities. All major decisions are made by the group as a whole. Each issue is discussed, then voted on by the members. After that, the executive, the manager and/or a committee is charged with carrying out the decision. Less important decisions may be made by the manager and/or the executive without a group vote. However, in these situations the manager and executive make concerted efforts to consult with as many members as possible.

d) Worker control – employee-directed

Comfort Clothing is also interested in co-operative structures and decision-making. It is attempting to implement a rather complex arrangement whereby workers and managers form the board of directors. Each employee has the right to vote for the employee – worker or manager – who she feels would make a good director. The board of directors, in consultation with other employees, then provide direction to management. At the present time, Comfort Clothing still has some board members who are community volunteers, although they are in the minority. The company uses an employee-directed 'management by committee' approach to its daily operations. Staff meetings are held weekly to discuss the actions of the board, agenda items for future board meetings, and regular operations.

e) The corporate model – board-directed

Some community economic development projects, such as Valley Woollen Mills, follow more traditional business practices. Elected board members set policies. Management reports to the board and has the responsibility for implementing board recommendations. At the board level, decisions are discussed and voted on. In most corporations, board members are elected by the shareholders or appointed by the existing board. Community economic development projects follow a similar pattern, although they can and do take liberties with the definition of 'shareholder'.

Principles of Decision-making:

a) Be thorough and decisive

It is important to get things done, because more than anything else, this will motivate people to continue working for your organization. However, it is just as important to ensure that decisions are well-informed, taking into account the needs of all parts of the organization. Thoroughness is difficult, but especially important in times of pressure. Since most community economic development projects experience a great deal of pressure, an effective decision-making process is not always easy to develop. Almost every project has had experience with decisions that have been made in too much haste.

> *"We rushed to get the wool out to the public . . . and it wasn't of equal quality to what people were already getting . . . It will take a while before we get their confidence again . . . We should have moved slower and involved the local women more in the development of our product."*
> – Member, Codroy R.D.A.

b) Maximize participation

When important decisions are being considered, it is essential to include as many members as possible. The more well-informed and concerned the people you involve are, the more ideas will be generated, and the better your ultimate decision will be. At your meetings, have the chairperson make special efforts to ensure that all discussions and proposals are understood, and that the members are sufficiently comfortable to discuss them. When members are absent from important discussions, someone should be delegated to visit or phone them. Sometimes, it may even be necessary to postpone a decision until the opinions of these people are known. Be prepared to accept these delays. Maximizing the participation of your members will lead to the growth of a strong and committed group.

c) Decentralize power and authority

Maximizing member participation will also help to ensure that the interests of the community are represented in your decision-making efforts. When all important decisions are made by a few people, these individuals inevitably become the most powerful. This will most likely lead to their particular interests dominating the group – possibly at the expense of other members.

d) Maximize for opportunity, not necessity

On the other hand, maximizing participation does not mean that everyone has to be involved with every decision. In fact, this approach has the potential to be very destructive.

> *"We've concluded that it's not a good thing . . . It's uncomfortable, unproductive to insist that everyone have an opinion on everything."*
> – Member, Is Five Foundation.

e) Involve those directly affected

The ideal situation seems to be one whereby all the people who are directly affected have input with regards to the decision-making process, and their needs are incorporated into the final decision. People who become involved with c.e.d. projects have to become masters of the 'art of compromise'.

f) Adopt an approach that fits your organizational structure

The purpose of your group and your organizational structure will influence your approach to decision-making. For example: a co-op will place emphasis on member votes; a small community business may operate as a collective, on a consensus basis; and a larger community business may choose to adopt a more traditional corporate model.

4. Problems with Communications and Decision-making

Most community economic development groups have spent a lot of time and energy trying to improve their communication and decision-making systems. Their skills, with few exceptions, are well-developed. However, problems involving poor communications or bad decision-making continue to crop up from time to time. They can never be eliminated entirely. Every community economic development group must be prepared to work at improving skills and resolving the conflicts that arise.

Typical Trouble Spots

1. Volunteers (feeling left out)
2. Informing the community
3. Efficiency (getting decisions made quickly enough)
4. Making and taking direct criticism

Virtually every project mentioned in this book has had problems with communications and decision-making. Is Five identified the orientation of volunteers as one of their weak areas. The NIDA project staff have had difficulties keeping the community at large informed. People from Comfort Clothing, Contact, the Mira Pasture Co-operative and the Codroy Valley R.D.A., mentioned difficulties relating to the actual responsibility for making decisions.

> *"We are a typical voluntary organization . . . We'd drag things on and on, talk till one in the morning and not reach a decision . . . hard for the employees to see why . . . It's frustrating for them."*
> – Board Member, Comfort Clothing Services.

> *"We don't like to hear things by the grapevine . . . if someone wants changes we like them to suggest them."*
> – Member, Mira Pasture Co-op.

Conflict Resolution

1. Find some common ground
2. Talk about it face to face
3. Form a committee
4. Develop a training programme
5. Build education/skill development into your plan

Having the perseverance and commitment to continuously work out these problems as they arise will significantly reduce their negative effects. Remembering that most people are not very articulate and what they say can easily be misinterpreted, is also important. Misinterpretations often lead to conflicts. When conflicts do arise, remember that there is usually more than one 'correct' interpretation of any event. Solving a conflict involves listening to each version, identifying the common ground, and reaching some form of compromise.

With serious conflicts, whether caused by poor communications or other reasons, it is best to resolve them by having the affected members talk it out face to face. If this approach is not successful, we recommend using a technique that has helped the Is Five group. Start by identifying the two members in the group who have the most widely divergent points of view. Then put the two opponents together on a two-person committee, with the objective of identifying a compromise solution.

If a group is not satisfied with its ability to communicate and make decisions, or is having continuous interpersonal problems, some form of education programme should be developed. This can be achieved in a formal or informal manner. Some groups have requested their local community college to design and organize a series of training workshops. Others have sponsored individual members at training sessions in other communities.

Still others have preferred to take an informal approach. Discussion groups at the local pub after work, or circulated reading materials, are some of the methods that have been used. Any of the above can be effective. The one you choose should be fitted to your group's interests and stage of development. For example, a workshop – involving the whole group and an instructor from a community college – may be a threatening idea to some of your members. A good discussion over beer might, in fact, be more effective.

Education/skill development of the membership is usually accepted more readily, if it is built into the project from the beginning and carried out on a continuous basis. When the CCEC was first established, for example, an education committee was formed to keep the membership informed about the credit union and the activities of other member groups. The committee has also supported or sponsored workshops, conferences and meetings where individuals could improve their skills and knowledge about running co-operative organizations.

ENTERPRISING COURSES

Community Business Training is a mutual endeavor of the New School for Democratic Management in San Francisco and a Vancouver based committee of volunteers. Many of those on the committee are members of food co-ops, workers' co-ops and other community organizations, and attend the New School courses in Seattle. It seemed overdue for a similar session to be brought to Vancouver – one that utilized more appropriate Canadian course content. All of our organizations needed skills, both technical and managerial, to further our goals and exercise our strength more effectively. The New School for Democratic Management offered those skills in a carefully developed package.

Remember the CCEC Economic Planning Conference last May? It generated a lot of interest amongst local co-operators who felt it was not enough to just meet with each other. They took the enthusiasm one step further and decided to sponsor a series of training sessions in Vancouver using New School for Democratic Management course content.

The New School has offered business training courses based on the principles of democracy in the workplace, since 1976. The premise is *"that it is more productive, and a better use of resources, to increase the authentic participation of employees in the running of organizations"*. The School seeks to make business education accessible to those who have never had it – community enterprises, co-ops, and non-profit organizations.

The session will take place February 20-24. Participants can choose up to three of nine courses offered at a cost of $65 for one, $120 for two, and $150 for three.

– CCEC Credit Union Newsletter, November 1979.

Not-for-Profit Management

The life span of your community economic development project will be determined in large part by the way in which it is managed. Management is the heart of any organization. It is also the area of c.e.d. where there are far more questions than answers. Although c.e.d. groups can learn a lot about how to organize and run their projects from conventional approaches to small business and to community organization, their 'not-for-profit' approach to business, and their 'business-like' approach to community development, create a unique situation. Many questions arise that cannot be adequately answered by conventional business practices or by the established traditions of community development.

The early history of co-ops and credit unions in Canada can be instructive with regards to c.e.d. management practices. Those co-operatives and credit unions attempted to develop structures that would allow for the operation of businesses with social consciences. However, the co-op model proved to have its failings, and for some groups, local co-ops provided more lessons about what not to do, than to do.

So the questions remain, and the whole process of organizing c.e.d. is still fraught with experimentation. For the most part, there are no straight answers to the questions that c.e.d. groups across Canada are asking about structure and management. There are, however, clear principles to follow. In addition, the trial and error process, which the groups interviewed for this book have all gone through, eventually produces some recognizable signs that indicate whether or not things are 'working' properly.

> *"Good management is essential . . . You just get at it. You take them [the employees] and make a team out of a bunch of individuals. That's good management."*
> – Employee, Valley Woollen Mills.

> *"We've got some problems now because we overlooked management training in our five-year plan."*
> – Member, Nimpkish Band Council.

There are two basic ways to organize: according to function; or by project. Most c.e.d. groups use a combination of both. The goal is to allow for maximum flexibility with minimum duplication of effort. Many organizations, for example, have a centralized office where one or sometimes two people handle bookkeeping, typing, phone calls and general community relations for all projects. Other work, however, may be handled on an individual, 'project' basis; in which case, resource identification, planning, some aspects of community relations, and business development work are done by the people responsible for that particular project.

The project-based organizational style is attractive since it avoids segmentation, encourages flexible and innovative thinking, allows for quick adjustments to programmes if necessary, and creates many opportunities for the kind of on-the-job training we mentioned earlier. The obvious disadvantage is that it is very easy to end up with a group in which everyone is off in a corner working by themselves – and opportunities to ask for, or offer, advice and expertise just do not present themselves.

Not only is this costly in terms of effective resource use; it can also breed feelings of insecurity, isolation and mistrust, as members of your organization lose their perspective of where they 'fit' and what their importance is.

In order to avoid this type of situation, community economic development groups make concerted efforts to bring members together. They sponsor social and recreational events (like picnics), or hold meetings, where members can discuss individual projects and issues that affect the entire group.

The management of c.e.d. organizations is never done by the manager alone. In fact, there may be no manager as such in your c.e.d. organization during its first years. Even in organizations that do have salaried positions, management tasks are shared by the staff, volunteers and board members. These tasks are listed below:

a) *planning*, in order to define desired results and the strategies that will make those results happen;
b) *organizing*, to establish a structure and mechanisms that will bring your plan into action;
c) *acquiring necessary resources* – both capital and technical assistance – in order to have the tools your organization needs to run smoothly;
d) *project assessment* – the evaluation of ideas for new profit-making projects;
e) *recruiting and co-ordinating volunteers and staff;*
f) *providing leadership and direction*, to fit the pieces of your organization together and ensure that they work smoothly;
g) *presenting your organization*, to your markets, community, peers and working partners in other communities; and
h) *evaluating and controlling your organization*, in order to assess its effectiveness and decide when it is time to 'spin off' a project.

The first five points have already been dealt with in this book. The remainder of this chapter will be spent discussing the additional 'management tasks' identified above.

Providing Leadership and Direction

When most people think of management, it is the leading and directing function that comes to mind. To provide appropriate leadership and direction is to combine technical, interpersonal and planning skills in order to create a smoothly functioning organization. It involves organizing and allocating work, making decisions, and co-ordinating the various parts of your organization. Like all other management tasks, leadership and direction comes not only from a manager, but also from board members, other employees and volunteers.

Presenting Your Organization

1. Developing your Markets

Marketing is an often neglected and crucially important aspect of project management. The basis of marketing is in the identification of needs, and the development of projects that provide services or products which respond to these needs. Marketing also links your organization to the outside world by: communicating information about your projects, and the benefits of the services or products you are offering; and establishing contact and developing relationships with the people who would be interested in, or who would benefit from, your services or products.

When we talk about the role of marketing in a c.e.d. organization, we are not just talking about advertising a product or service. Community economic development organizations do of course advertise and publicize their projects and enterprises. However, they also market their organizations to potential private and public funders, and to members of their own communities. The key to c.e.d. success is through proper marketing: of products and services to clients or customers; and of the organization itself to the community it serves and to sources of potential support.

In order to market effectively, every c.e.d. organization needs to develop ways of gathering information on a regular basis, concerning:

a) who the organization actually serves, and how this fits in with your goals;
b) what changes are taking place in 'community needs';
c) how should the organization respond to these needs; and
d) publicity and promotion – i.e. finding out what kind of information is best for conveying the purpose, goals and activities of your organization to different target groups, such as clients and customers, community members, potential funders, or groups/organizations that are sources of mutual support.

Collecting and using this kind of information are essential practices, if good planning and financial success are to be components of your c.e.d. organization.

2. Developing Relationships

It is essential for your organization to build relationships with individuals and groups who are in a position to provide support to your project.

Who Should You Look For?

a) Local residents

Your local community is always your most important source of support. Local people, and the resources they control, must be the 'heart and soul' of your project. However, this is not to say that outside groups and organizations are not important. They too have a role to play in the functioning of your c.e.d. project – e.g. people from other c.e.d. projects, government resource and funding groups, or business associations.

b) Other c.e.d. projects

One of the blessings of having a good working relationship with other c.e.d. projects is the understanding that will exist between you. Very few individuals or outside organizations will be able to grasp what you are really attempting to accomplish as easily as another community economic development group.

c) Government organizations

Government organizations are also important groups to establish working relationships with. They cannot provide the 'peer' support that other c.e.d. projects can, but they are important sources of information. Research, policy developments and support programmes relating to your project's goals are important areas to keep track of. If you have personal contacts with people in government, the civil service and the organizations that advise government (e.g. Science Council of Canada), you will have a better chance of getting accurate and up-to-date information.

These contacts will also be of assistance to you when your organization is making proposals for government support. They can ensure that your proposal is understood; they can sometimes even make presentations on your behalf. Government officials usually feel more comfortable about community projects they are familiar with, especially if there is a member of parliament or a senior civil servant vouching for its credibility. In these situations, it is essential that you have someone on the 'inside' who can help you.

However, at the same time, you must not allow yourself to become labelled as a group that is 'owned' by one particular political party. Such a development could significantly reduce your ability to solicit resources from people who are not members of that group. It could even destroy the credibility of the project itself.

The solar panels on the Community Alternative Society's Co-op Building were built with a loan from CCEC.

d) Business groups

Business groups (like regional business associations), or national groups (like the Federation of Independent Businesses), can also be important sources of support and information. Although there will be significant differences between your group and other private sector businesses, there will also be many areas of common interest. This will be especially evident in the case of other small, independent businesses. For example, Is Five is presently working with a firm that builds trucks. They are 'partners' in the design and testing of a truck capable of 'picking up' glass and paper for recycling purposes. Sources of venture capital, improved government tax policies, and ideas for improving management are examples of other interests you will have in common.

Businesses will also provide supplies for your own projects – and possibly become customers as well. Business groups, like most interest groups, are biased towards businesses they are familiar with. Personal contacts and relationships are some of the most important aspects of 'doing business'. It is essential, therefore, that the people involved with c.e.d. ventures develop close contacts with the business community.

How to Build Relationships:

The first step, of course, is to build your own group into an effective organization. Outsiders will judge you by what you have accomplished. Your active supporters will come from local activists and leaders – the people who get things done. These people are usually busy, and will only give their time to groups that are committed to achieving something and are capable of doing so.

a) Identify community leaders

Once your group is established and functioning effectively, you can begin to build a 'community support system'. When you were 'getting started', you identified who the community leaders were, and what groups would act as allies. If your information is up-to-date, use it; if not, you will need to update it.

b) Identify community organizations with mutual interests

Identify which groups have related interests, and a basis whereby you could work together. For example, most c.e.d. projects have problems with funding and management. Each has had some successes, as well as some failures. By getting together, you can share experiences and possibly assist each other with specific problems – e.g. as the CCEC credit union has done. Some of the ideas being explored by c.e.d. groups include: sharing facilities and equipment; joint purchasing; and a policy of buying goods and services from each other before going to private sector businesses.

Clearly identify what your complimentary interests are, and how they can be developed. Establish what these outside organizations can do for you, and what you can do for them. Throughout the book, we have stressed this principle of 'mutual aid'. It is important to use it when developing relationships as well. You will probably have to make the first move. *Be prepared to be the 'ice-breaker'.*

c) Take the first step

Community economic development groups generally work in a quiet fashion. The groups and individuals they are interested in contacting are usually sent some written material (e.g. a brochure and/or letter), that describes the project. This is then followed by a request for an appointment, or an invitation to a small meeting or social gathering. The specific approach varies according to the people you are trying to establish contact with, or the type of relationship you are trying to build. Business people often prefer a brief, one-on-one meeting. On the other hand, a local community organization might prefer an informal workshop, where you could present your group's plans. *Regardless of what approach you choose, always keep in mind that the first step will have to be made by you.* You are the 'new kid on the block' – an organization that most people probably have difficulty understanding.

> *"There are people in this area who think the Rural Development Association isn't worth a damn . . . People here are very independent and suspicious of anything new."*
> – Member, Codroy R.D.A.

The 'Unfair' Competitor

There have been a few occasions when a community economic development project has been viewed as an unfair competitor by local businesses and/or social service groups. These groups have objected to c.e.d. projects on the basis that they receive public funds; or conversely, because they run businesses – and therefore 'cannot have' social goals. These conflicts usually arise when the purpose of the c.e.d. project has been misunderstood, and/or these outside organizations have a basic disagreement with the philosophy behind community economic development. It is important for your organization to minimize this type of conflict by keeping the local community informed, and by establishing good working relationships with other groups. The members of your organization must help the local community to understand that your project's purpose is to assist the development of local businesses and social services – i.e. to make them more viable. You are not there to interfere with existing organizations that are effectively serving the community. In addition, it is important for the community to understand that community economic development projects solicit public funds on the same basis as any other business or social group.

d) Test the water

Once you have met and identified areas of mutual interest, test out your new relationship by doing something for each other. Enhance your chances of success by choosing an activity that is small and simple. If possible, avoid complicated or long-term projects until you are well-acquainted with one another. However, this is only a 'rule of thumb'; exceptions do occur. Community economic development projects often share facilities or loan equipment as a first step in building a relationship. Supplying information to a government official, in exchange for having a meeting arranged with a cabinet minister, is an example of how you can 'test out' working with a public official. Trying to get small business tax policies changed, by co-sponsoring conferences or briefs to government, could help your businesses as well as improve your credibility with other private sector groups. If these first efforts are fruitful, do not hesitate to move onward – i.e. maximize the potential of the relationship.

Informing Your Community: Your relationship with your community will develop along different lines from your relationships with specific groups – i.e. it will be a more open, public process. Once your organization has been established, you should begin to keep the community informed about what you are doing. For example, have an open house or a community meeting. These events are also good ways to identify potential new members for your organization.

Potential Difficulties: Developing good relationships outside your organization is never easy. It is an area that has to be carefully nurtured and managed. Often the people you want to associate yourself with are spread throughout a very large area. This alone makes contact difficult and expensive. In every c.e.d. project, there always seems to be a 'bush fire' that needs attending to; this leaves little time for visiting outside contacts. In addition, some of your external relationships will not be directly related to your work. Therefore, they will be important to your organization, but not a priority.

You can minimize your difficulties by making sure your organization is well-managed, and your priorities clearly established. Establishing contacts and building working relationships are important aspects of c.e.d. work, and can be valuable resources. However, their potential value can only be realized if you are clear about your priorities and stick to them. It is not wise to spend much time developing external relationships during the early stages of your project.

It is essential that external relationships be dealt with in a strategic manner. Wait until your own organization is well-established locally. When you are ready, keep yourself informed about as many outside organizations and government departments as possible. Be on their mailing lists and make periodic requests for information. However, be selective. Concentrate on creating a few well-developed contacts. Try to establish contacts with groups that can be of direct assistance to you. People involved with c.e.d. find their spare time very limited. Therefore, time spent on activities not related to your project's priorities has to be limited as well.

SUMMARY: Principles of Building Relationships

1. Build your own group into an effective organization.
2. Concentrate on building a few well-developed contacts.
3. Identify community leaders and organizations with interests similar to yours.
4. Be prepared to take 'the first step' – go out and explain the purpose of your organization and how it functions.
5. Be sensitive to being perceived as an 'unfair competitor'.
6. All relationships should be built on a principle of 'mutual aid'.
7. When you have identified a potential partner, plan a joint project.
8. Your first co-operative effort should be small and simple.

Evaluation and Control

1. Use a Plan

Your plan is the major tool used in evaluating and controlling the performance of your organization. Not only should there be a plan to cover your organization's overall activities, but each project should also have its own individual plan – stating its goals and objectives, activities, budget, schedule, and expected sources of capital and technical resources.

2. Check the Plan Regularly

Control in your organization means checking the plan regularly in terms of your actual activities. Most organizations have regular meetings to look at how they are doing. Check your performance as an organization against your schedule of activities, and against your projected revenues and expenses. Are you on schedule? Are you within your budget? Are your activities meeting the goals and objectives they were designed for? What is your basis for deciding? What changes should be made to your plan and to your activities? When will these changes be effective? How will you know?

3. Evaluate Objectives, Not People

It is important to evaluate projects rather than people. It is always best to talk about people's contributions in terms of the objectives of a project, rather than in terms of their personal strengths and weaknesses. Of course, a poor performance should not be ignored. The earlier it is confronted, the better. A change in workload, a transfer of responsibility or some extra training can sometimes prevent a resignation or firing later on.

4. Establish Evaluation Processes Early

One of the burdens of receiving grants is the 'evaluation procedures' that often accompany them. When you accept a grant, be sure to find out in detail which evaluation procedures are expected, and which indicators will be used. Negotiate any changes right away. If you wait until it comes time to produce the results of the evaluation to try to make changes in the methodology, you are likely to run into difficulties.

5. The Meaning of Success

No one will really be able to tell you how to evaluate your c.e.d. programmes. 'Success' has so many different meanings that it is impossible to establish general criteria to apply to every c.e.d. project. Detailed studies can sometimes be helpful in evaluating your progress, but few c.e.d. projects have the resources to undertake such studies. The best approach is to measure your accomplishments against certain factors. What these factors are depends on what is important to your community. Often, they include things like the:

a) number of jobs created;
b) number of people involved in various community activities;
c) revenues generated;
d) types of assistance given to other organizations and businesses; and
e) extent of community support for projects.

6. 'Spinning Off'

The concept of 'spinning off' is central to community economic development. One of the lessons learned from the co-op movement is that the larger an organization becomes, the more difficult it is to remain community-based and community-run. Community economic development organizations recognize, that in order to remain truly community-based, they must remain small. However, c.e.d. is also a 'developmental process', and in order to retain this side of its nature, it must continue to respond to changing community needs.

The solution to the need to be small, but growing, can be found in the idea of 'spinning off'. Once a project is well-established – i.e. financially self-sufficient, with well-developed management skills – it is ready to be spun off. Once the parent c.e.d. organization has developed new projects that generate sufficient revenues, it can afford to spin off more mature projects.

Maintaining Ties

When a project spins off, it becomes independent – a separate organization. Ties to the parent organization are maintained in various ways:

a) the 'parent' may hold a minority equity position, or hold membership in a co-op arrangement;
b) interlocking boards of directors;
c) partnership efforts in projects of mutual interest;
d) contracting back and forth for goods and services; and
e) maintaining affiliative ties – e.g. being part of the same support network, and acting as friends and advisors to one another.

Giving up control is never easy for either party. Accepting the responsibilities of an independent operation is often difficult. This is about as much as we know, for in Canada, few c.e.d. organizations have been through the spinning off experience. However, it seems that the basic principles of c.e.d. generally apply to spinning off. Only time and experimentation will tell for sure.

How to 'Spin Off' a Project

The principles of c.e.d. suggest that spinning off should take place in the following manner:

1. It should be well-planned and take place in identifiable stages.

2. It should be collaboratively planned.

3. It should take place gradually.

4. The 'parent' should be prepared to carefully define and maintain limited ties for long periods of time – often for more than five years.

5. The former project should have the ability to adjust and change those ties at its own discretion.

6. Care should be taken to develop enough internal support within the former project, so that it does not become necessary for the 'parent' to take over in times of crisis.

7. Flexibility must be built into the plan. Changes – some radical, always unexpected – are likely to be necessary.

8. Consideration must be given to the fact that if a project is successful, private and public sector interests will want to take it over. If community ownership is a continuing goal, you must watch this situation carefully. In some communities, take-overs – particularly by the private sector – may be just what local people are hoping for. In these cases, the need to ensure community control is less urgent.

Some Final Comments

Community economic development in Canada is still very young. There are few signs yet as to what the 'second generation' should or will look like. Hopefully, books written a few years from now, will be able to use current c.e.d. experiences as the basis for a better analysis of spinning off than we can provide at this time.

> *"In order to prove that it works, you've got to give it away . . ."*
> – Member, Is Five Foundation.

> *"This mill has taken more than enough of our time, but we'd never unload it until it was viable. Just like Peckford, we want to develop it the way we see it . . . We'll be able to have the mill viable within the next year. Then, I don't know . . . Maybe we'll set up a co-op or something, with controlling interest by the R.D.A. – I don't know . . ."*
> – Member, Codroy R.D.A.

> *"It'll be a good feeling* [*in the future*] *for those who've been involved. . . It would be hoped that the next generation would take it* [*the pasture*] *over. Things like that have a way of carrying on somehow."*
> – Member, Mira Pasture Co-op.

For Further Reading:

Canadian Council on Social Development, *Tapping the Untapped Potential: towards a national policy on volunteerism*, Ottawa, 1977.

Institute for New Enterprise Development, *Building Skills for C.D.C. Boards: notes for a board training committee and its consultants*, Cambridge, Mass.

A Few Last Words

We live today in an uncertain world. Events on the other side of the globe – in places like Iran, Afghanistan and South Africa – influence our daily lives as Canadians. Yet we have little opportunity to understand, much less control, that influence. Politically and economically our country moves with the same winds of change as other countries around the world. Issues such as the use of nuclear power, the rising cost of food and the vulnerability of an oil-based industrial structure reach far beyond our border. In Canada and other industrialized countries, advances in technology mean that fewer and fewer people are needed to 'run the world'. The relationship between people, their tools and the product of their work has been altered in a way that alienates them from the product of their efforts.

This situation is not good. Many jobs are alienating. The sense of productivity – of creating something meaningful and useful – is absent. There is also the other aspect of the problem – i.e. that fewer people are employed. Fewer jobs are necessary. Technological innovations such as word processing, which promises to eliminate literally thousands of jobs in the service sector, mean that the economic mainstream – industrial society – has a diminishing number of places within it for paid employees. For many people, there are no jobs – alienating or not – available.

At one time planners told us not to be concerned. Alienation at work could be counterbalanced by new and productive uses of leisure time. For those who do not have jobs, the surplus wealth created by the efficiency of industrial society would supposedly provide adequate support. However, while this vision of the future may work for a few people, for most it has no meaning. Alienation at work, or no work at all, does not generally result in increased motivation to make productive and creative use of available time. Apathy, poverty and social problems seem to be the more common results. The so-called 'welfare mentality' is one, given deprivation of opportunity, that can affect us all.

At one time government leaders told us that publicly-sponsored economic development efforts were bringing us closer and closer to a national goal of full employment. These days, despite many such programmes, we hear little about full employment. Nor do we hear that by putting up with a certain degree of unemployment; we can hold inflation in check. As unemployment figures and inflation rates continue to rise, we mostly hear that ways to regain control of the economy must be found soon.

The truth is that government has no solutions for us. It, like the industrial private sector, is bound by a narrow view of the 'economy' that precludes all solutions but those which have already been found wanting. From the private sector we continue to hear assurances that further corporate development will benefit us all, in spite of generations of evidence to the contrary; and from the public sector, we hear only new variations of the same old strategies that have long since ceased to be effective.

Left without direction from the 'experts', it is more and more apparent that new solutions will have to come from a new direction – from the ordinary people in society. The problem then lies not with 'new' national economic policies and development strategies, but rather with finding adequate ways to make a living. The issue becomes not whether or not to provide support to a weakened industrial structure, but how to build local self-reliance.

Most communities are not wealthy. Their supply of available local resources – human and material – is limited. Much is absorbed by the economic mainstream in terms of money, materials and expertise. At first glance, it might seem unreasonable to expect new solutions from such a limited source. It is certainly true that for communities engaged in their own economic development, the work is not easy. Every success is built on what has been learned through previous mistakes and failures.

However, successes do occur. Experiments are going on all across Canada. New solutions are emerging. What communities have – that the 'experts' do not – is a perspective that is based on life as it occurs day-to-day. Community economic development goals are never to increase the GNP or to increase incentives for regional growth. The purpose of c.e.d. is not to make a profit. The field of vision of people in community economic development is not defined by available economic theory. They have come to realize that community survival needs a solid economic base, but people involved in c.e.d. are not just working at it because it's their job; they work at it because they want a home – a place to live and work for themselves and their children.

What makes c.e.d. different from other economic development strategies is that it endeavours to place this economic base in the hands of those to whom it means the most – the people for whom it makes community life possible. Despite verbal commitments to local self-help efforts by governments in Canada and around the world, there has been little evidence of actual support. Skepticism about the ability of ordinary people to do what's best for them continues to thrive in 'high' places. However, in the face of increasing evidence of the potential of community-controlled efforts and a lack of alternatives, it may not be long before mainstream economic thinkers 'find' a 'new' solution – something called community economic development.

Of course, c.e.d. is not the only solution. The economic problems of the world's best-behaved colony will not be solved by any one strategy of economic development. Community economic development, as we have tried to point out in **Community Profit**, is only feasible under certain circumstances.

Community economic development efforts will always be small and decentralized. They will be successful only in communities that have some access to local resources. Their impact will never be large or sudden.

However, other strategies are necessary too. Much is still unknown about c.e.d. in Canada. Most projects are less than ten years old. It will be some time before we know just what the place of c.e.d. – and the whole third sector – will be. Whatever its future, though, community economic development has certainly earned a place in Canadian development thinking. It cannot be ignored.

For Further Reading:

Burns, Scott, **The Household Economy: its shape, origins and future**, Boston, Beacon Press, 1977.

Illich, Ivan, **Tools for Conviviality**, New York, Harper & Row, 1980.

Robertson, James, **The Sane Alternative**, London, Villiers Publications, 1978.

Schumacher, E.F., **Small is Beautiful: economics as if people mattered**, New York, Harper & Row, 1975.

Index to Resources

The following index is a list of organizations/programmes, which were identified as being of some use to community economic development groups in Canada by the people we interviewed while writing **Community Profit.**

LOCAL AND OTHER COMMUNITY RESOURCES

1. **Canadian Library Association,** 151 Sparks St., Ottawa, Ontario, K1P 5E3. Libraries are a potential source of information for various types of projects. Major libraries have good access to government statistics and information describing existing programmes.

2. **Universities, Community Colleges, (C.E.G.E.P.)**
Although for the most part these institutions do not appear to provide the valuable assistance they are capable of, four of the projects described in this book had an active relationship with a local college and/or university:
   a) Memorial University of Newfoundland, Department of Extension, St. John's, Newfoundland, A1C 5S7.
   The Extension Department has several field workers. One of them has worked with the Rural Development Association in Codroy.
   b) College of Cape Breton, Bras D'Or Institute, Sydney, Nova Scotia, B1P 6L2.
   The Institute has provided research support for Mira Community Pasture and New Dawn Enterprises.
   c) St. Lawrence College, Department of Student and Community Services, Portsmouth Ave., Kingston, Ontario, K7L 5A6.
   The department was active in the initial planning and organizing work of Comfort Clothing Services.
   d) North Island College, 156 Manor Rd., Comox, British Columbia.
   The field staff of North Island College have sponsored continuing education courses (e.g. small business management) in co-operation with the Nimpkish Band Council.

3. **Municipal Governments**
Some municipalities have been active supporters of community-based

projects. The City of Toronto is presently considering an assistance programme and the city government in Halifax has been an active supporter of the Human Resources Development Association.

4. **Canadian Co-operative Credit Society**, Box 800, Stn. 'V', Toronto, Ontario. Credit unions were initially established to be community-based financial institutions. The credit unions that have retained a 'community orientation', are often a valuable source of technical assistance in the area of financial management. From time to time, they will also provide small grants for special community projects. In some provinces, the 'Credit Union League' will also sponsor training programmes in financial management and co-op development.
   The address of the 'Credit Union League' can be obtained from any local credit union. The Co-operative Union of Canada will also provide information: Co-operative Union of Canada, 237 Metcalfe Ave., Ottawa, Ontario.

5. **Recycling Council of Ontario (R.C.O.)**, 467 Richmond St. E., Toronto, Ontario, M5A 1R1.
   R.C.O. is a fledgling organization, representing the recycling groups in Ontario. Like its counterparts in other provinces, e.g. British Columbia, R.C.O. will provide written information and advice on recycling including its benefits as an economic resource.

6. **PLURA**, c/o 14 Brooklyn Ave., Toronto, Ontario M4M 2X5.
   A church-based organization representing the people of the Presbytarian, Lutheran, United, Roman Catholic and Anglican churches. PLURA is a small group which has clearly identified 'grass root' community groups from poor and isolated communities as their priority. PLURA provides small grants which can be used towards operating costs.

7. **Service Clubs** – see *Canadian Almanac and Directory*; Walters, Susan, ed., Copp, Clark, Pitman; Toronto, 1980.
   Most non-native communities have locally organized service clubs. The Lions Club, Kiwanis, and Rotary are familiar examples. In some communities, these organizations have a history of active support for projects directed towards community betterment. Often, they are the community's expert fund raisers.

8. **Frontier College**, 31 Jackes Ave., Toronto, Ontario, M4T 1E2.
   For more than eighty years, this private college has been working in remote Canadian communities. As a recipient of a 'UNESCO Award,' Frontier has achieved world-wide recognition as a leader in adult education and literary work. During recent years the college has also become directly involved in community education and community-based economic development.

9. **Canadian Executive Services Overseas (C.E.S.O.)**, 1130 Sherbrooke St. W., Montreal, Québec.
   C.E.S.O. volunteers are executive level professionals, who work as volunteers in the 'Third World' and with native groups in Canada.

10. **Unions** (e.g. United Steelworkers, United Auto Workers).
    Local unions have been used as a source of assistance. Their members can

provide valuable technical expertise to your group and be a source of project funds. Financial support is usually restricted to projects which directly affect the well-being of their members.

11. **United Way of Canada**, Place de Ville, No. 915, 112 Kent St., Ottawa, Ontario.
The United Way is an organization which represents and raises funds for its member groups. Member groups usually are sponsors of community-based development projects or service projects which cannot receive total funding from the government. In many communities, the United Way is the largest source of non-government money available to non-profit community organizations.

THIRD SECTOR RESOURCES

Across Canada, there are many community economic development projects. They are located in every province, in large and small communities. Although some first efforts at creating a national organization have begun, at this time there are no federal or provincial community economic development organizations. The best way to locate other community economic development groups in your region is still by word of mouth.

In **Community Profit**, we have referred to several community economic development projects in addition to the ones described in detail in Chapter 2. They are briefly described below:

1. **CJRT-FM**, 297 Victoria St., Toronto, Ontario.
CJRT is a non-profit radio station in Toronto. While not strictly speaking a community economic development organization, in that it exists solely to provide radio services, it is a good example of a not-for-profit business in a highly competitive environment. Commercial radio stations in Toronto support CJRT because it provides a service which they approve of but are not able to provide themselves.

2. **Human Resources Development Association (HRDA)**, HRDA Enterprises Ltd., 1730 Granville St., Halifax, Nova Scotia, B3J 1X5.
Initiated with support from all 3 levels of government, HRDA is a community economic development organization that attempts to work closely with local agencies and institutions in creating employment for people whose usual source of income is social assistance payments. The province of Nova Scotia and the City of Halifax both divert money from their social assistance budgets to provide partial support for operating costs.

3. **Community Employment Strategies Association (CESA)**, c/o Ron Ryan, Guysborough, Nova Scotia.
Formerly a federal Community Employment Strategies project, CESA is now using a federal one-time grant of $500,000 as a source of development and venture capital. A separately incorporated holding company has been created to carry out this function.

4. **Co-operative d'Amenagement des Ressources du Transcontinental (CART)**,

c/o Gérard Peron, L'ecole secondaire de Sully, Sully, Québec.
CART is an association of community economic development projects, in eastern Québec.

5. **Nanaimo Community Employment Advisory Society (N.C.E.A.S.)**, 124 Nicol St., Suite 2, Nanaimo, British Columbia, V9R 4S9.
N.C.E.A.S. was formed in 1975 as part of the federal Community Employment Strategies programme (CES). When CES was phased out, N.C.E.A.S. began to search for ways to continue its work and develop a secure funding base. N.C.E.A.S. created a separately incorporated holding company. The holding company, provides venture capital and technical assistance to local enterprises using a $500,000 one-time grant from the federal government to provide the start-up funds for its capital pool.

6. **New Dawn Enterprises Ltd.**, P.O. Box 1055, Sydney, Nova Scotia, B1P 6H7.
Started in 1974, New Dawn is one of Canada's best known and oldest community development corporations. Starting with the acquisition and renovation of a building in order to provide a home for the Cape Breton School of Crafts, New Dawn has continued to use real estate and construction as the economic means by which it accomplishes a wide variety of social and cultural ends. Each of three divisions – social, cultural and business – sponsor a range of activities and connected organizations, all under the New Dawn umbrella.

7. **United States – Community Economic Development**
In the United States, there are two divisions of community economic development organizations: federally-sponsored 'Title 7' community development corporations, of which there are about forty; and non-'Title 7' groups which receive support from a variety of federal and state programmes, of which there may be as many as 800.
Information regarding community economic development in the U.S. can be obtained through:
a) National Congress for Community Economic Development, 2025 Eye St. NW, Washington, D.C., 20006.
b) Centre for Community Economic Development, 1320 19th St., NW, Washington, D.C., 20036.
c) Institute for New Enterprise Development, 17 Dunster St., Cambridge, Massachusetts, 02138.
In addition, there are numerous consultative organizations which specialize in research, project planning, and training. Two of these organizations have worked with projects mentioned in this book:
– Institute for New Enterprise Development (worked with New Dawn).
– New School for Democratic Management, 589 Howard St., San Francisco, California, 94105 (worked with CCEC).

PRIVATE SECTOR RESOURCES

The availability of private sector resources varies widely from community to community. Below are listed a few organizations which have links with communities all across Canada.

1. **Chamber of Commerce,** Canadian Chamber of Commerce, Commerce House, 1080 Beaver Hall Hill, Montreal, Québec, H2Z 1T2.
The Chamber of Commerce is an organization of business people who work to support and promote businesses in their own communities. They often are a good source of local trade information. Contact your local Chamber of Commerce or the national office in Montreal.

2. **Chartered Banks**
Canada's chartered banks are offering more and more services to small businesses. The Royal Bank and the Bank of Commerce both emphasize 'community banking' – the provision of banking services to small communities and have an expressed interest in serving the needs of small businesses.

3. **Corporations** – see *Canadian Almanac and Directory*; Walters, Susan ed., Copp, Clark, Pitman; Toronto, 1980.
The magazine, *Canadian Business*, publishes an annual list of Canada's 500 largest corporations. The *Globe and Mail* (Toronto) every year produces a special business section which summarizes annual reports and offers a distribution service to its readers for annual reports from major corporations. Unlike their American neighbours, Canadian corporations do not publish information concerning corporate donations to non-profit organizations. As a result, such information can best be gained by word of mouth.

4. **Canadian Association of Management Consultants**, Suite 615, 1243 Islington Ave., Toronto, Ontario, M8X 1X9.
A listing of management consultants is published by the Canadian Association and is available in most libraries.

5. **Foundations** – see *Canadian Directory to Foundations and Granting Agencies*; Walters, Susan ed., Copp, Clark, Pitman; Toronto, 1980.
Foundations which have shown a particular interest in supporting innovative Canadian developments include: Atkinson (Ontario only), Bronfman (e.g. native people and publications), Donner (e.g. native peoples, economic development), Ford (e.g. local economic development). Also see *Resources for Community Groups*, published by the Ontario Ministry of Culture and Recreation, for a listing of foundations interested in community-based efforts.

6. **Better Business Bureau of Canada, Inc.**, 2 Bloor St. E., Suite 3034, Toronto, Ontario, M4W 3J5.
Located in most cities, the Better Business Bureau branches are supported by their member businesses. The goals of the Better Business Bureau are to promote ethical and fair business practices. They operate public information services, offering advice and information and investigating complaints.

7. **Canadian Federation of Independent Business**, 15 Coldwater Road, Don Mills, Ontario, M3B 3J1.
Organized to promote and support small business in Canada, the C.F.I.B. has proven to be an effective and forceful lobby group. It also offers information about small businesses to members.

8. **Canadian Co-operative Credit Society**, Box 800, Stn. 'V', Toronto, Ontario. See Local and Community Resources.

PUBLIC RESOURCES

Many public programmes – provincial, federal and local are potentially available to community economic development projects. Below are listed only those which the projects described in Chapter 2 have used:

Federal Government

1. **Canada Employment and Immigration Commission (CEIC)** – often known as Manpower. Employment Development Branch, Ottawa, Ontario, K1A 0J9.
   Although CEIC's programs are not designed with community economic development groups in mind, they are a primary source of financial assistance for projects in Canada.
   Information on the following programs is available from your local 'Manpower' Centre or your provincial CEIC office, Employment Development Branch:

   a) Canada Community Development Programme (formerly LIP, formerly Canada Works.)
   b) Canada Community Services Programme.
   c) Young Canada Works.
   d) Local Employment Assistance Programme (LEAP).
   e) Local Employment Development Associations Programme (LEDA).
   f) New Technology Employment Programme (N.T.E.P.).
   g) Community Employment Strategies Programme (CES), no longer operating.
   h) Economic Growth Component Programme, no longer operating.

Assistance with the costs of employee training and development is available through:
   a) Canada Manpower Industrial Training Program (C.M.I.T.P.).
   b) Training in Business and Industry (TIBI).

2. **Department of Regional Economic Expansion (DREE)**, Ottawa, Ontario, K1A 0M4.
   In conjunction with the provincial governments, DREE has identified regions in Canada where the local economies need government assistance. Each province negotiates an agreement with DREE to determine where and how DREE should assist local communities. 'Special ARDA' is one of DREE's programmes designed to provide assistance to native groups. 'Special ARDA' is available in selected regions of the country.

3. **Energy, Mines and Resources (E.M.R.)**, Conservation and Renewable Energy Branch, Ottawa, Ontario.
   In recent years, this federal department has sponsored several programmes related to community energy problems, e.g. DRECT.

4. **Department of Industry, Trade and Commerce**, 235 Queen St., Ottawa, Ontario, K1A 0H5.

This Department has several programs designed to assist Canadian businesses. The staff also can also be a valuable source of information with regard to business projects and markets.

5. **Department of Indian and Northern Affairs**, Economic and Social Development Branch, Ottawa, Ontario, K1A 0H4.
   The primary assistance programme for native people interested in community economic development is the Indian Economic Development Fund.

6. **Federal Business Development Bank (F.B.D.B.)**, Public Affairs, 280 Albert St., Ottawa, Ontario, K1P 5G8.
   The F.B.D.B. is a federally sponsored organization, established to assist entrepreneurs with viable ideas, who are unable to obtain financing from private lending institutions. F.B.D.B. is also a source of information on business development and management. Several reports and handbooks are available free of charge on request. In addition, F.B.D.B. administers the CASE (Counselling Assistance for Small Enterprise) programme. CASE is a low-cost business counselling service available to small businesses. The consultants are often retired businessmen.

7. **National Health and Welfare**, Welfare Grants, Brooke Claxton Building, Tunney's Pasture, Ottawa, Ontario, K1A 0R9.
   Under the Welfare Grants programme, Contact and New Dawn were given five and three year grants to demonstrate the potential of the community development corporation idea.

8. **Secretary of State**, Assistance to Community Groups, Terasses de la Chaudière, 15 Eddy St., Hull, Québec, K1A 0M5.
   Each regional office has at least one person responsible for this programme. Staff are able to offer their time as advisors to community organizations, and occasionally provide small grants to specific community projects.

9. **Katimavik** – OPCAN, 323 Chapel St., Ottawa, Ontario.
   This programme sponsors projects across Canada in conjunction with local organizations. Projects focus on community betterment and provide young people with work experience in a community away from home.

10. **Habitat** (no longer functioning)
    In connection with an international conference sponsored by the United Nations and hosted by the federal government of Canada and the provincial government of British Columbia, communities were invited to submit proposals for demonstration grants.

PROVINCIAL RESOURCES

Although the jurisdictions of each province are the same, their ways of structuring them and dividing up their rights and responsibilities differ greatly. Each province has responsibilities for social services, education, and recreation. In some provinces programmes initiated in these areas can provide resources to community economic development groups, in others they do not. This varying commitment to community economic development will probably continue into the future. It appears that while some provincial governments are preparing to provide significant assistance, others are not. In addition to Newfoundland's existing Rural Development Programme, Québec, Saskatchewan (Department of Northern Saskatchewan, Economic Development Branch) and Ontario (Ministry of Industry and Tourism, Small Business Development Branch) have shown interest in launching new initiatives.

Below are listed provincial resources which have been used by the seven organizations described in this book:

a) British Columbia, Salmon Enhancement Programme, Fish and Wildlife Branch, 1019 Wharf St., Victoria, British Columbia.
   Operated through contracts with the provincial Department of Recreation and Conservation, the Salmon Enhancement Programme is designed to improve the quantity and quality of B.C.'s salmon stocks.

b) Newfoundland, Department of Rural Development.
   The Department of Rural Development, through the DREE agreement, provides small yearly operating grants and several other support services to local Rural Development Associations.

c) Nova Scotia.
   The Mira Pasture Co-op was able to obtain a land-clearing grant through the Department of Lands and Forests. The Ministry of Agriculture has provided advice and some technical assistance. The Cape Breton Development Corporation, created through a DREE agreement, was able to provide the Mira co-op with a small loan, and the loan of some equipment on a short-term basis.